Essential
Orlando

by Emma Stanford

Emma Stanford has written books and articles
on Florida, California, the Caribbean, Hawaii,
France and Spain, as well as Mediterranean
port guides for the US navy. She has also
contributed to guides published by the BTA,
American Express and Fodor.

AA Publishing

Above: *live at Gatorworld*

Page 1: *Wet 'n' Wild*

Page 5a: *face-painting at Lake Eola Park*
5b: *Southern belle, Cypress Gardens*

Page15a: *whale at Sea World*
15b: *posing at JFK Space Center*

Page 27: *gourmet food*
27b: *Busch Gardens*

Page 91a: *King Henry's Banquet, International Drive*
91b: *showtime at Rosie O'Grady's*

Page 117a: *taxi driver*
117b: *Monument to the States, Kissimmee*

Find out more about AA Publishing and the wide range of services the AA provides by visiting our Web site at www.theaa.co.uk.

Written by Emma Stanford

Edited, designed and produced by AA Publishing.
© The Automobile Association 1998
Maps © The Automobile Association 1998

Distributed in the United Kingdom by AA Publishing, Norfolk House, Priestley Road, Basingstoke, Hampshire, RG24 9NY.

A CIP catalogue record for this book is available from the British Library.

ISBN 0 7495 1636 4

Published by AA Publishing, a trading name of Automobile Association Developments Limited, whose registered office is Norfolk House, Priestley Road, Basingstoke, Hampshire, RG24 9NY.
Registered number 1878835.

Colour separation: BTB Digital Imaging Ltd, Whitchurch, Hampshire

Printed and bound in Italy by Printers Trento srl

Contents

About this Book

Essential *Orlando* is divided into five sections to cover the most important aspects of your visit to Orlando.

Viewing Orlando pages 5–14
An introduction to Orlando by the author.
Orlando's Features
Essence of Orlando
The Shaping of Orlando
Peace and Quiet
Orlando's Famous

Top Ten pages 15–26
The author's choice of the Top Ten places to see in and around Orlando, each with practical information.

What to See pages 27–90
The three main areas in and around Orlando, each with its own brief introduction and an alphabetical listing of the main attractions.
Practical information
Snippets of 'Did You Know...' information
5 suggested tours
2 features

Where To... pages 91–116
Detailed listings of the best places to eat, stay, shop, take the children and be entertained.

Practical Matters pages 117–24
A highly visual section containing essential travel information.

Maps
All map references are to the individual maps found in the What to See section of this guide.
For example, Busch Gardens has the reference ✚ 46A1 – indicating the page on which the map is located and the grid square in which the attraction is to be found. A list of the maps that have been used in this travel guide can be found in the index.

Prices
Where appropriate, an indication of the cost of an establishment is given by **£** signs:
£££ denotes higher prices, **££** denotes average prices, while **£** denotes lower charges.

Star Ratings
Most of the places described in this book have been given a separate rating:
✪✪✪ Do not miss
✪✪ Highly recommended
✪ Worth seeing

Viewing
Orlando

Emma Stanford's Orlando

*Dolphins working out at
Sea World*

Getting Around
Short-stay visitors can tackle
Orlando without a car, though
public transport is pretty
sketchy. Most hotels offer
free shuttles to Walt Disney
World, and Orlando's
International Drive resort area
has the cheap and efficient I-
Ride trolley bus (7AM–
midnight, stopping every two
blocks between Sea World
and Belz Factory Outlet mall).
For longer stays, independent
transport is a worthwhile
investment, opening up a host
of alternative day trips to the
Gulf coast or Atlantic beaches,
state parks and other Central
Florida attractions.

Orlando really is the town that Mickey Mouse built. A
former cattle ranchers' watering hole and citrus depot in
dusty Central Florida, the quiet country town boomed after
the opening of the first Walt Disney World theme park,
Magic Kingdom, in 1971. Today, Orlando is firmly established as one of the world's top holiday destinations.

More than 36.5 million visitors pour into Orlando every
year; over the past quarter century, over 500 million have
visited Walt Disney World. The sheer volume of interest in
Orlando has meant that the city has grown fast – often too
fast for developers to concern themselves with the
niceties of landscaping or public transport – and the main
tourist areas have spread out well beyond the confines of
Orlando itself. Many visitors to Walt Disney World, a 30-
minute drive south of International Drive, choose to stay in
the neighbouring town of Kissimmee. However, what
Orlando may lack in aesthetic urban planning it more than
makes up for in thrills, spills and Disney magic. This is
theme park heaven boasting state-of-the-art rides, family
entertainment and fantasy on tap. Add gratifyingly high
standards of service and you have a holiday destination
that could teach the rest of the world a thing or two.

Orlando's Features

Distances
• Distance from Miami: 236 miles
• Distance from New York: 944 miles
• Distance from Los Angeles: 2,203 miles
• Distance from London: 4,336 miles

Size
• Population: 175,000 (City of Orlando); 1.1 million (Greater Orlando)
• Population density: 4,000 people per square mile
• Annual visitors: 36.5 million

Geography
• Latitude: N 28° 32'
• Longitude: W 81° 22'
• Height above sea level: 70 feet

Climate
• Warmest months: July–August (high 92°F, low 73°F)
• Coolest month: January (high 72°F, low 49°F)
• Wettest month: July (7.8 inches of rain)
• Driest months: November–December (1.8 inches of rain)

Top: *the impressive Orlando skyline*
Above: *catching the surf on the Atlantic coast*

Facilities
• Hotel rooms: 84,000
• Restaurants: 3,000-plus
• Visitor attractions: 66
• Golf courses: 123
• Tennis courts: 800
• Watersports: 300-plus inland lakes, springs and rivers for fishing, swimming and boating; an hour's drive from the Atlantic and Gulf coasts
• Spectator sports: basketball (Orlando Magic); baseball (spring training); ice hockey (Orlando Solar Bears); roller hockey (Orlando Jackals); American football (Orlando Predators)
• Retail shopping space: 32 million square feet
• Transport: Orlando International Airport is the 18th busiest in the US (26th in the world), with more than 1,000 flights daily serving 100 cities worldwide

As You Like It
There are two versions of how Orlando came to be named. One credits pioneer settler and local big-wig, Judge V D Speer, with having named the town after a character in his favourite Shakespeare play, *As You Like It*. The other is that the town was named after Orlando Reeves, a US soldier killed by an Indian arrow in 1835, while raising the alarm to save his company, in what is now downtown Orlando's Lake Eola Park.

7

Essence of Orlando

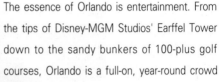

Below: *doing the can-can at Rosie O'Grady's*
Bottom: *fun on the rapids at Busch Gardens*

The essence of Orlando is entertainment. From the tips of Disney-MGM Studios' Earffel Tower down to the sandy bunkers of 100-plus golf courses, Orlando is a full-on, year-round crowd pleaser. Visitors can share their breakfast muffins with Goofy and the gang, lunch in Splendid China, get whisked aboard a Magic Carpet at the Arabian Nights dinner theatre and never really set foot in Florida. But this would be a mistake. Beyond the man-made wonders, Central Florida offers sparkling lakes, citrus groves, lovely gardens and a rich and varied wildlife showcased in relaxing state parks.

THE 10 ESSENTIALS

If you only have a short time to visit Orlando, or would like to get a really complete picture of the region, here are the essentials:

- **Magic Kingdom:** the 'must see' classic Disney park (➤ 82–7). Another Disney classic is the Mouse Ear hat (8 million sold since 1971).
- **T2 3-D:** the hottest theme park thrill to arrive in recent times, Universal Studios' Terminator 2 'virtual adventure' sneaks a 3-D march on its rivals (➤ 42).
- **Manatees**, or sea cows, are the endangered gentle giants of Florida's waterways. If you cannot get to see them in the wild (➤ 51), do not miss Sea World's Manatees: The Last Generation? (➤ 38).
- **Do the birdwalk**, a little-known secret: the Gatorland marsh boardwalk is one of the best birdwatching spots in the region (➤ 32).
- **Blooming marvellous:** for local horticultural colour, enjoy the formal delights of Leu Gardens (➤ 32), or the woodland trails of Bok Tower Gardens (➤ 47).
- **Silver Spurs:** cattle ranchers first settled the area in the 1840s and Kissimmee celebrates its origins with the bi-annual Silver Spurs Rodeo (➤ 60).
- **Drink up!** Florida produces around 75 per cent of the nation's citrus crop, so be sure to sample fresh local juices.
- **Shop 'til you drop:** the top end of Orlando's International Drive has turned into a magnet for bargain-hunters, with factory outlet stores galore (➤ 105).
- **Look into the future:** forget sci-fi for a moment and head Behind the Seeds at Disney's Epcot Center for a fascinating look at the future of agriculture (➤ 77).

Above: *fresh Florida oranges*
Below: *enjoying the show at Fort Liberty*

- **Doing dinner** can be quite an event in Orlando. A host of popular dinner theatres offers themed evenings from Medieval Times to 1930s-style Capone's (➤ 113).

The Shaping of Orlando

Spanish explorer Juan Ponce de León found Florida while looking for the fountain of youth

1513
Spanish explorer Juan Ponce de León discovers Florida.

1565
Pedro Menéndez de Avilés, Captain General of the Spanish treasure fleets, founds St Augustine on the Atlantic coast, the oldest continuously inhabited European settlement in the US.

1763–83
The British occupy Florida for 20 years before it is returned to Spain under the Second Treaty of Paris.

1817–18
Tensions between the incoming white settlers and native American Seminole Indians spark the First Seminole War.

1819
Spain relinquishes Florida to the US in settlement of a $5 million debt.

1835–42
Second Seminole War. Fort Gatlin established close to present-day Orlando c 1837.

1842
The US army escorts 3,000 Seminole Indians on the 'Trail of Tears' to exile on reservations west of the Mississippi. Settlers move into Central Florida.

1843
Cattleman pioneer Aaron Jernigan arrives from Georgia, and constructs a stockade on the shores of Lake Holden. The early settlement in the vicinity of Fort Gatlin is named Jernigan in 1850.

1845
Florida achieves statehood.

1857
Jernigan is renamed Orlando (see panel on ► 7). Local settlers make their living from cattle-ranching and cotton.

1861
Florida is the third state to secede from the Union and join the Confederacy. Start of the Civil War (1861–5).

1865
WH Holden plants Orlando's first

commercial citrus plantation on his 100-acre property. At first the fruit has to be hauled overland to Sanford and then carried by boat to markets in Charleston, SC.

1875
The City of Orlando (all 2 square miles of it), county seat of Orange County, is officially incorporated by a vote of 22 men from the total population of 85.

1880
Henry Plant's South Florida Railroad links Kissimmee/Orlando to Tampa on the Gulf coast.

1890s
English settlers buy up land around Orlando for around $1 an acre and plant citrus.

1894–5
The Great Freeze devastates Central Florida's citrus groves. Faced with ruin, the English settlers are rumoured to have consoled themselves by playing cricket. Meanwhile, orange-grower John B Steinmetz converts his packing house into a skating rink with picnic facilities, a toboggan slide and a bath house, creating Orlando's first visitor attraction.

1922
First cargo planes land at Orlando, followed by passengers in 1928.

1929
Mediterranean fruit fly attacks citrus orchards in the Orlando area. The National Guard are called out to enforce quarantine regulations and spray the infected crop, and the threat is eradicated within a year.

1956
The Glenn L Martin Company of Baltimore (now Lockheed Martin) annouces plans to build a missile factory in Orange County, giving a considerable boost to the local economy together with the proximity of the new Cape Canaveral aerospace complex.

1965
Walt Disney announces his plans for Walt Disney World.

1971
The first phase of Walt Disney World, Magic Kingdom, opens.

1977
The last orange grove on Orlando's famous Orange Avenue is bulldozed to make way for a shopping centre.

1983
Epcot Center opens.

1989
Disney–MGM Studios opens. The three Walt Disney World theme parks comprise the world's number one tourist destination.

1990
Universal Studios opens.

1998
Walt Disney World opens Animal Kingdom, its fourth full-size theme park.

1999
Universal Studios plan to unveil a second theme park, Islands of Adventure, and a full vacation resort complex.

The space shuttle Discovery *taking off*

Peace & Quiet

Escaping the hustle and bustle of Orlando's theme parks and non-stop fun is not only an attractive idea but essential if you are spending more than a few days in town. Though Central Florida is not renowned for its scenery – undulating citrus groves are the main feature – it is remarkably easy to step back from the concrete jungle and discover pockets of wild, undeveloped natural Florida just around the corner.

Water, Water Everywhere

There are more than 300 named lakes and dozens of rivers, ponds and springs in the vicinity of Orlando, offering excellent bass-fishing, boating and swimming opportunities. They also act as a magnet for wildlife, particularly waterbirds such as herons, snowy egrets, coots, gallinules and the bizarre-looking anhinga bird, which swims with its body beneath the surface and only its long, thin, snake-like neck protruding.

Below: *taking life easy: there are plenty of boating opportunities in Orlando*
Inset: *the unusual anhinga or 'snakebird'*

A boat tour of Lake Tohopekaliga, in Kissimmee, is a great way to get away from it all, and there is a good chance of spotting bald eagles and osprey, as well as more common species. Tours depart from the marina and there are boats and fishing tackle for hire (▶ 61). There are also scenic boat trips on Winter Park's lakes, where wildlife plays second string to expensive lakeshore real estate, but the odd alligator occasionally surfaces to give passengers a thrill for their money (▶ 67).

Nature Trails

Within easy reach of Orlando, there are more than half-a-dozen state parks giving access to unspoilt wilderness, marshland boardwalks and nature trails for wildlife-spotting, as well as canoe runs, fishing lakes and picnic grounds in a natural setting. North of Orlando, the sand pine woods of Ocala National Forest are one of the last refuges of the Florida black bear and home to barred owls and wild turkeys. A 66-mile section of the cross-state Florida National Scenic Trail runs through the forest, and there are numerous shorter trails, while canoe runs, such as Juniper

Leu Gardens, a wonderful haven of peace in downtown Orlando

Springs, are reckoned to be among the best in the state (▶ 62).

For winter visitors to picturesque Blue Spring State Park, on the St John's River, there is the added incentive of spotting a manatee (▶ 51). You could combine a nature walk with a visit to the beach on a day trip to Merritt Island National Wildlife Refuge and the Canaveral National Seashore, in the shadow of the Kennedy Space Center launch pad on the Atlantic Coast (▶ 58).

Glorious Gardens

If nature in the raw does not appeal, there is peace and quiet to be found in a brace of delightful gardens. Just north of downtown, Leu Gardens is a tranquil lakeshore spot boasting one of the finest camellia collections in the US (▶ 32). The shady woodlands of Bok Tower Gardens, near Lake Wales, make a soothing escape, where the only sound to disturb the birdsong is the chimes of the famous carillon (▶ 47).

Orlando's Famous

Osceola, champion of the Seminoles, pictured in about 1830

Osceola

A charismatic warrior and the principal native American leader of the Second Seminole War, Osceola (c1803–38) settled near the Peace River south of Orlando in around 1808. Utterly opposed to the forced migration of Seminole Indians to reservations west of the Mississippi, Osceola's hostility towards white settlers and the US government was further inflamed by the kidnap of his wife, Che-cho-ter (Morning Dew), whose trace of Negro blood allowed her white captors to claim she was a fugitive slave. After executing a Miccosukee chief for accepting government money to migrate, Osceola led an attack on Fort King which triggered the outbreak of war in 1835. Public outcry greeted Osceola's unlawful capture while negotiating under a flag of truce in 1837, but he was held in St Augustine and transferred to Fort Moultrie, South Carolina, where he died.

Zora Neale Hurston

Celebrated Black folklorist and writer Zora Neale Hurston (1903–60), was born and raised north of Orlando, in Eatonville, one of the first incorporated Negro towns in the US. Employing the language of the rural Black south, she wrote evocatively of her people. Her mostly widely acclaimed novel, *Their Eyes Were Watching God*, was published in 1937, and an autobiography, *Dust Tracks on a Road*, in 1942.

Mickey Mouse

Mickey Mouse was born in California in 1928 (see panel). He made his first screen appearance that year in *Steamboat Willie*, and went on to star in more than 100 cartoon movies, including a challenging role as the Sorcerer's Apprentice in *Fantasia* (1940). Mickey and his companion, Minnie, established a base in Florida in 1971 and also have homes in France and Japan.

A Star is Born
As a teenager living in Kansas, the man behind the Mouse, Walter Elias Disney (1901–66), took a correspondence course in cartoon-drawing. When a successful early cartoon character, Oswald the Lucky Rabbit, fell victim to an unscrupulous distributor, Disney returned to the drawing board and created Mortimer Mouse, inspired, so the story goes, by the field mice that used to frequent his old Kansas City studio. The mouse was renamed Mickey by Disney's wife, Lillian. The rest is history.

Top Ten

1
Busch Gardens

Hold on for a stomach-churning ride

The combination of exotic animals, thrilling roller coasters, water rides and shows makes this one of Florida's top attractions.

Busch Gardens lies around 75 minutes' drive west of Orlando, in Tampa. Opened in 1959, it is a seasoned crowd-pleaser with pleasantly mature grounds shaded by trees and flowering shrubs. The overall plot is 'Africa', with 10 themed areas such as Nairobi, Timbuktu and the Serengeti Plain; the latter incorporates the brand new Edge of Africa domain, inaugurated in the summer of 1997.

The 335-acre park houses one of the nation's premier zoos. There are more than 2,800 animals from over 300 species wandering the grassland enclosures of the Serengeti Plain, inhabiting the rocks and waterfalls of the Great Ape Domain and featured in other displays such as the Bird Gardens. Busch Gardens plays a significant role in breeding and conserving endangered species and many of the zoo's latest additions are proudly displayed in the Nairobi Animal Nursery.

But animals are by no means all the park has to offer. In honour of the 1996 International Year of the Roller Coaster, Busch Gardens unveiled Montu, the tallest and longest inverted roller coaster in the world. The Kumba ride remains among the largest and fastest steel roller coasters in existence, and the water rides provide varying degrees of thrills and spills, and a chance to cool off in the Florida sunshine.

Small children are particularly well catered-for here. In addition to the animal attractions, there is the interactive Land of the Dragons play area, and colourful ice shows in the Moroccan Palace Theater. Strollers are available for rental in the Morocco district; there is a full baby-changing and nursing area in Land of the Dragons.

See also ➤ 48–50.

✛ Off map 46A1

✉ Busch Boulevard, Tampa (75 miles west of Orlando via I-4 West and I-75 North to Fowler Avenue/Exit 54)

☎ (813) 987 5082

🕐 Daily 9:30–6 (extended summer and hols)

🍴 Refreshment stops throughout park, plus the full-service Crown Colony Restaurant (Crown Colony) (£–££)

♿ Very good

✋ Very expensive

❓ Check daily schedules for show times

2
Church Street Station

In the heart of downtown Orlando, an old railway depot has been transformed into a first-class entertainment complex.

Part of the much needed downtown rejuvenation project commenced in the 1970s, Church Street Station offers one-stop shopping, dining and entertainment in a collection of fine old red-brick buildings decorated with ironwork balconies. This is the place to come for a spot of shopping followed by an evening of Dixieland jazz or thigh-slapping Country and Western music, a romantic dinner, a night dancing to rock and roll classics or the latest disco sounds.

The complex comes in two parts: the Exchange Building, which houses the attractive Victorian-style shopping mall of 50 or so specialist boutiques and stores, and the majority of the restaurants and showrooms; and the Brumby Building, across the street, where the remainder are located.

Apart from the undoubted quality and variety of entertainment on offer at Church Street (➤ 30–1), the complex's other claim to fame is its meticulously restored 19th-century interiors furnished with original antiques. Dotted about the four spectacular showrooms, the restaurants and other entertainment areas are huge, hand-carved Viennese mirrors, Victorian brass chandeliers, a bar made from an 18th-century French communion rail and a wine cabinet bought from a Rothschild house in Paris. Perhaps most impressive of all is the magnificent Western-style Cheyenne Saloon and Opera House, which took two and a half years to construct from over 250,000 board feet of golden oak lumber from a century-old Ohio barn.

✚ 29C3

✉ 129 W Church Street (I-4 to Exit 38/Anderson Street)

☎ (407) 422 2434

🕐 Daily 11–2; The Exchange shops 11–11

🍴 Lili Marlene's (££–£££); Cheyenne Saloon Barbeque Restaurant (££); Crackers Seafood Restaurant (££); Rosie O'Grady's Deli (£); Exchange Food Court (£)

♿ Good

✋ Expensive; tickets cover admission to all showrooms for the whole evening. Admission to The Exchange shops: free

❓ Check schedules for special events and the annual St Patrick's Day, Halloween and New Year's Eve Street Parties

Eating, shopping and entertainment all in one

3
Cypress Gardens

<table>
<tr><td>✚</td><td>46B1</td></tr>
<tr><td>✉</td><td>State Road 540 W, 4 miles east of Winter Haven (off US27, 22 miles south of I-4)</td></tr>
<tr><td>☎</td><td>(941) 324 2111 or 1-800 282 2123</td></tr>
<tr><td>🕐</td><td>Daily 9–5:30 (extended summer and hols)</td></tr>
<tr><td>🍴</td><td>Crossroads Restaurant & Terrace (£–££); Cypress Deli (£); Village Fare Food Court (£); assorted snack and refreshment stops (£)</td></tr>
<tr><td>♿</td><td>Very good</td></tr>
</table>

Florida's first theme park remains faithful to its botanical origins and is famous for its four annual flower festivals.

Sloping gently down to the shores of Lake Eloise, near Winter Haven, a 45-minute drive south of Orlando, Cypress Gardens was originally laid out in the 1930s along the swampy water's edge, shaded by giant cypress trees. The park has expanded considerably since, covering more than 220 acres, and offers a variety of shows, shopping, dining and animal attractions in addition to the carefully manicured gardens, eye-catching topiary and other horticultural exhibits.

For plant-lovers, the lush Botanical Gardens remain the highlight of a visit. Shaded brick paths meander through dense tropical plantings of heliconias and bromeliads, cascades of brilliantly coloured bougainvillea and forests of

Cypress Gardens, colourful at any time of the year

<table>
<tr><td>🤚</td><td>Very expensive</td></tr>
<tr><td>↔</td><td>Bok Tower Gardens (► 47), Lake Wales (► 61)</td></tr>
<tr><td>❓</td><td>During high season reservations are advised for Pontoon Lake cruise (additional fee) and Botanical Boat Cruise</td></tr>
</table>

bamboo. There are acres of formal gardens, too, and for sheer spectacle it is hard to beat the Spring Flower Festival, November's Mum Festival, featuring more than 2.5 million chrysanthemum blooms, and the winter holiday Poinsettia Festival.

Flower power aside, Cypress Gardens takes pride in its water-ski revues on the lake, and the 153-foot-high Island in the Sky revolving observatory. At its foot, Southern Crossroads houses snack stops, restaurants and shops.

Recent developments in the park concentrate on the wonders of the natural world, with the Butterfly Conservatory and Nature's Way area featuring a walk-through aviary, animal enclosures and a wooden boardwalk area on the lake.

See also ► 52.

4
Fantasy of Flight

Vintage planes, each with a story to tell, help illustrate aviation history at this new Central Florida attraction.

The first thing to notice at Fantasy of Flight are the elegant 1930s and 1940s-style Art Deco themed buildings, designed to capture the spirit of aviation's Golden Era. Within the twin hangars and parked out on the runways are more than 20 vintage aircraft, just a part of the world's largest private collection built up over the last 20 years by aviation enthusiast Kermit Weeks.

The earliest authentic aircraft on display here, including a Sopwith Camel, date from World War I. However, illustrating the real dawn of flight, there is a reproduction of the Wright Brothers' 1903 Kitty Hawk Flyer, a cat's-cradle of wires and wooden struts, which has actually flown – if only for a few seconds at a time. A prime Golden Era exhibit with a notable history is the 1929 Ford Tri-Motor, launched by movie star Gloria Swanson. It flew across the US coast-to-coast in 48 hours and was later used in the making of *Indiana Jones and the Temple of Doom*.

The collection of World War II fighter planes from the US, Britain and Germany are among the museum's most popular exhibits, and visitors can test out their air combat skills in the Fightertown Flight Simulators, piloting their way through an aerial dogfight over the Pacific. Another themed 'immersion experience' is the History of Flight, with its walk-through dioramas recreating significant events, from balloon trips to a bombing mission aboard a World War II B-17 Flying Fortress.

See also ➤ 53.

➕ 46A1

✉ SR-559, Polk City (I-4 West to Exit 21)

☎ (941) 984 3500

🕐 Daily 9–5 (extended summer and hols)

🍴 Compass Rose (£–££)

♿ Good

✋ Moderate (additional charge for Fightertown Flight Simulators)

Fantasy of Flight, where the past comes to life

5
Kennedy Space Center

47D2

✉ State Road 405, Merritt Island (Bee Line Expressway/SR528 toll road east from Orlando)

☎ (407) 452 2121 or 1-800 572 4636

🕐 Daily 9–dusk

🍴 Mila's Roadhouse Grill (£–££); cafés and concessions (£)

♿ Very good

✋ Admission: free. Bus tours: moderate. IMAX film shows: cheap

❓ Bus tours depart at 9:30, then every 15 minutes (allow 2½ hours). Book for the IMAX cinemas at Spaceport Central on arrival

Tours, films, rockets and space hardware bring the American space programme to life at NASA's Florida space launch facility.

The Kennedy Space Center's Visitor Center is the gateway to Launch Complex 39, where today's space shuttles blast off into orbit, and where Apollo 11 set off on its ground-breaking journey to deliver the first man to walk on the moon in 1969. A visit to the Space Center offers a terrific opportunity to delve into the history of the US space programme, experience a nail-biting re-creation of the countdown to blast off, get a behind-the-scenes view of space technology and look at the possible shape of things to come.

The very first rockets launched from Cape Canaveral were long-range guided missiles fired from Cape Canaveral Air Force Station in the early 1950s. NASA, the National Aeronautics and Space Administration established in 1958 to carry out the peaceful exploration and use of space, later used the site to prepare and launch science satellites and the manned and unmanned flights of the early Mercury and Gemini programmes. In 1964, NASA trans-ferred operations to Launch Complex 39, at Merritt Island, which was designed to handle the Apollo-Saturn V programme. The first launch from the Kennedy Space Center was the Apollo 8 mission in December 1968.

The Space Center, now one of Florida's top visitor attractions, has recently added the spectacular new $37-million Apollo/Saturn V Center. To make the best of a visit, plan an itinerary which includes a bus tour and at least one of the stunning giant-screen IMAX films. Families with small children will probably find a half-day visit long enough.

See also ➤ 59.

The Space Shuttle exhibit comes highly recommended

6
Sea World

Shamu, the killer whale, star of Sea World, heads up an all-star cast at the world's most popular sea life park.

A walrus steals the show at Sea World

Laid out over an action-packed 200-acre site, Sea World provides a full day's itinerary of shows and marine encounters in the best theme park tradition. The stars of the shows are almost exclusively of the finned or flippered variety and their virtuoso performances (coaxed by the strategic deployment of a seemingly endless supply of fish) are a source of continuous amazement and delight to packed audiences. Though Sea World can get very busy, its built-in advantage over other traditional parks is the almost complete absence of rides, so there are few queues. This is good news, particularly for families with small children.

Shamu shows, performances in the Whale & Dolphin Stadium and the Sea Lion & Otter Stadium are a must. The Penguin Encounter (with real snow) should not be missed, and anybody who has never seen a manatee should rectify this immediately, and then sign up to help rescue these gentle and endangered Florida seacows.

Not surprisingly, Sea World pushes its role as a significant animal rescue, conservation and research facility. By and large the claims ring true, and the aquariums and outdoor enclosures appear adequate for animals often bred in captivity; but the jury is still out on the Wild Arctic exhibition and the desirability of importing polar bears and beluga whales to Florida. See also ➤ 38–9.

✚ 46B2

✉ 7007 Sea World Drive, Orlando (I-4/Exit 27-A or 28)

☎ (407) 351 3600

🕐 Daily 9–7 (extended summer and hols)

🍴 Aloha Polynesian Luau (£££); Bimini Bay Cafe (£–££); Buccaneer Smokehouse (£); Chicken'n Biscuit (£); The Deli (£); Mama Stella's Italian Kitchen (£); Mango Joe's Cafe (£); Smokehouse Chicken & Ribs (£); Waterfront Sandwich Grill (£)

🚌 I-Ride, Lynx #42

♿ Very good

✋ Very expensive

7
Silver Springs

Boat trips, jeep safaris, animal encounters and popular music shows are all part of the deal at 'Florida's Original Attraction'.

All aboard the Silver Queen

 46A4

 SR40, 1 mile east of Ocala (72 miles northwest of Orlando)

📞 (352) 236 2121 or 1-800 234 7458

🕐 Daily 9–5:30 (extended summer and hols)

🍴 The Deli (£); Springside Pizzeria (£); Springside Restaurant (£–££); Swampy's Smokehouse Buffet (£–££); snack stops, ice creams and cold drinks stalls (£)

♿ Good

✋ Very expensive; no extra charge for concerts

↔ Ocala National Forest (► 62)

In 1878, Silver Springs entrepreneur Hullum Jones had a brainwave. He installed a glass viewing box in the flat bottom of a dugout canoe and invented the glass-bottomed boat tour, hence this popular nature park's claim to being the Sunshine State's first tourist attraction.

More than a century on, the glass-bottomed boat rides are as popular as ever, creating a window into an under-water world teeming with fish, turtles, crustaceans and ancient fossils at the head of the world's largest artesian spring formation. Visitors can also enjoy the Lost River Voyage which plies the unspoilt Silver River, with a stop at a wildlife rescue outpost; or a Jungle Cruise on Fort King Waterway, where non-native animals look on.

Jeep safaris also do the jungle thing, four-wheeling through a 35-acre Florida jungle, where specially designed animal habitats include an alligator pit. A new attraction, opened in 1997, is the World of Bears.

Showtime at Silver Springs brings on the bugs and the creepy-crawlies at Creature Feature, an alarmingly up-close look at spiders and scorpions, toads and giant Madagascan hissing cockroaches. For something a little more wholesome, watch domestic cats and dogs performing tricks at the Amazing Pets displays. The park also attracts popular music acts for its annual weekend Concert Series starting in March.

See also ► 63.

8
Splendid China

Sixty of China's best-known scenic, cultural and historic sites have been re-created in meticulous miniature at this 76-acre site.

Inspired by a similar park laid out in the southern Chinese city of Shenzen, Splendid China is a masterpiece in miniature. It took 120 Chinese artisans two years to complete the project, using traditional craft methods dating back to the 14th century. The beautifully finished models of pagodas and palaces, and the half-mile-long one-tenth size version of the Great Wall, used up more than 6.5 million tiny bricks.

The craftsmen also built a scaled down army of Terracotta Warriors, based on the famous terracotta figures discovered guarding the tomb of the Qinshihuang emperor at Xi'an in 1974. The four-storey-high Leshan Grand Buddha Statue is a dainty replica of the 235-foot-high original which is carved into a mountain and can accommodate 10 men on each of its toes. Take a stroll around a fragment of the 65,765-acre petrified limestone Stone Forest found in Yunnan Province, and marvel at the elegant Summer Palace where hundreds of colourful ceramic supplicants, soldiers and courtiers crowd the courtyards, and royal barges load up from marble jetties on the edge of a lagoon landscaped with twisted, lichen-spotted dwarf trees.

Splendid China is also famous for its shows featuring Chinese acrobats and dancers, such as the 90-minute Mysterious Kingdom of the Orient spectacular, which takes place in the Golden Peacock Theater in the evening.

See also ▶ 65.

🚩 29A1

✉ 3000 Spendid China Boulevard/NM 4.5, Kissimmee (3 miles west of I-4/Exit 25-B)

☎ (407) 396 8880 or 1-800 244 6226

🕐 Daily 9:30–7 (extended summer and hols)

🍴 Within park: The Great Wall Terrace (£–££); Wind and Rain Court (£–££); Pagoda Garden (£). Chinatown shopping area: Seven Flavours (£); Hong Kong Seafood Restaurant (£££)

♿ Very good

✋ Very expensive

↔ A World of Orchids (▶ 46)

❓ Guided walking tours and tours in motorised carts can be arranged for a fee

China's fabled Imperial Palace in the Forbidden City, re-created in miniature

9
Walt Disney World

🕂 29A1

✉ Walt Disney World,
Lake Buena Vista (I-
4/Exits 25-B and 26-B,
20 miles south of
Orlando)

☎ (407) 939 7727

🕐 Check current
schedules

🍴 Each park offers a wide
choice of dining options
open for breakfast,
lunch, dinner, and
snacks throughout the
day. Priority seating
(bookings service at
Guest Relations) is
advised for table service
restaurants (££–£££)

🚌 Free shuttle bus
services from many
Orlando/Kissimmee
hotels

♿ Excellent

✋ Very expensive

❓ Details of daily parades,
showtimes and
nighttime fireworks and
laser displays are
printed in current park
guides. Tickets are
available on a one-day,
one-park basis. Savings
on the Four-Day Value
Pass (one park each
day) and Four-Day Park-
Hopper Pass (any
combination of parks
each day), covering the
three main parks, are
minimal. For longer
stays, the Five-Day
World-Hopper Pass is
good value, allowing
unlimited entry to all
main theme parks and
water parks

This is the big one: Walt Disney's Florida showcase put Orlando on the map and has become a legend in its own short lifetime.

The Walt Disney World Resort is the largest and most famous theme park resort in the world. Its 30,000-acre site is twice the size of Manhattan, and although only a small portion of this has been developed to date, it already contains the three major theme parks, Magic Kingdom, Epcot Center and Disney-MGM Studios, with a fourth, Animal Kingdom, due to open in 1998, plus three water adventure parks, a nightclub theme park, 27 themed resorts, shopping villages, gardens, lakes, five championship golf courses and a professional sports complex.

Walt Disney opened his first theme park in Anaheim, California, in 1955. Disneyland, the prototype for the Magic Kingdom which now flourishes in Japan and France as well as Florida, was a huge success, but Disney was unable to control the explosion of hotels that popped up around the site and prevented him from expanding the park. Instead, he began to look for alternative locations and was drawn to Orlando for its climate, communications links and vast tracts of cheap farmland, which he began to purchase in secret during 1964. With 28,000 acres in the bag at a cost of around $5.5 million, Disney announced his plans to create 'a complete vacation environment' unsullied by low rent commercialism.

Disney died in 1966 without seeing his Florida vision completed. But the Disney Corporation did him proud producing Magic Kingdom in Disneyland's image. This opened in 1971, followed by Epcot (Experimental Prototype Community Of Tommorrow), a futuristic pet project devised by Disney which finally opened its doors in 1985. Disney-MGM Studios was rushed out in 1989, months ahead of Universal Studios' mammoth Florida facility (➤ 26); and now Central Florida's animal-orientated parks are preparing to feel the pinch as Walt Disney World adds Animal Kingdom to its ever-expanding list of attractions.

'Doing Disney' is quite an undertaking. There is so much to see that it is all too easy to overdo things, and first time visitors are in danger of wearing themselves out with ambitious plans to see the lot in a couple of days. Take a tip from the repeat visitors who plan their itineraries with almost military precision, zero in on the best rides and avoid the restaurants at peak times. Never plan on doing more than one park a day, and if you are visiting all three parks during your stay, include at least one rest day.

Cost is another important consideration: Disney does not come cheap. If money is no object, the Walt Disney World Resort is without doubt the best place to stay with a choice of fine hotels boasting excellent facilities and free transport to the parks. Package deals paid in advance to cover theme park tickets and accommodation in the Walt Disney World Resort hotels are one way of avoiding a nasty shock. For budget travellers there is plenty of affordable accommodation near by in Kissimmee, or around Orlando's International Drive.

See also ➤ 69–90.

Cinderella Castle, Walt Disney World's most famous landmark

10
Universal Studios

✝ 29B2

✉ 1000 Universal Studios Plaza, Orlando (I-4/Exit 29 or 30-B)

☎ (407) 363 8000

🕐 Daily from 9AM; closing times vary

🍴 17 cafés, burger bars, ice cream parlours (£), and restaurants including Lombard's Landing (££); Hard Rock Café (££); Louie's Italian Restaurant (£–££)

♿ Very good

✋ Very expensive

↔ Wet 'n' Wild (➤ 43)

Filming a New York street scene

A ticket to ride the movies, Universal Studios is a favourite with fans of blockbuster rides, shows and attractions.

Back in the silent movie era, Universal Studios boss Carl Laemmle inaugurated the first movie studio tours at his Hollywood Hills facility in California. Opened in 1990, Universal Studios Florida is now the world's number one movie studio-cum-theme park, boasting more than 40 rides, shows and attractions; and the 444-acre complex is set to more than double in size with the unveiling of the Universal City Florida vacation resort, incorporating a second theme park, Islands of Adventure, in 1999.

In the meantime, there is no shortage of things to do and see at Universal Studios. Heading the pick of the rides is the 21-million jigowatt Back to the Future...The Ride with its stomach-churning, backbone-crunching simulator action. There are further tremors of terror in Earthquake – The Big One, and Kongfrontation. The latest absolutely unmissable adventure is Terminator 2: 3-D Battle Across Time, a super-sophisticated combination of live action and special effects.

In between rides, there are entertaining shows drawn from hit movies such as Beetlejuice and The Blues Brothers, powerboat and Wild West-type stunt shows. The studios of children's television channel Nickelodeon is another favourite diversion. Junior visitors from overseas enjoy the anarchic humour and gurgling green slime geyser just as much as their US contemporaries.

After dark, Universal's laser show is visible for miles around. The park also features specially themed events, from the springtime Mardi Gras celebration, with floats direct from the famous New Orleans parade, to Fourth of July, Hallowe'en and New Year.

See also ➤ 40–2.

What To See

Orlando

In the 1930s, traffic signals in downtown Orlando wore a sign admonishing drivers to be quiet. There were fresh fruit juice stands on the sidewalk and the city resembled 'a great, cultivated park'. Since Orlando has become synonymous with theme parks, it is generally assumed to be a loud, brash place.

Living in the shadow of the Mouse has certainly brought radical changes. The mini-Manhattan of the downtown district is bounded by highways, and the sky is busy with jets coming to and going from the international airport. But the city of Orlando has not succumbed entirely to the trappings of the tourist industry. There are pockets of greenery in downtown Lake Eola and Leu Gardens, and recent developments have included the renovated historic district around Church Street Station, a sleek new Science Center and the palatial 1.1 million square-foot Orange County Convention Center.

> *'Orlando has been a favorite resort for a type of visitor … [who] believes his health and longevity depend upon orange juice and the local brand of sunshine.'*

The WPA Guide to Florida
(1939)

Orlando

Orlando's untidy outline sprawls either side of I-4, the fast interstate highway which slices across Central Florida from the Gulf of Mexico to the Atlantic.

The city has extended steadily southwest towards Walt Disney World and Kissimmee, and most visitors who stay in Orlando are based south of the city in the International Drive resort area. Sea World and Universal Studios are just off I-Drive (as International Drive is familiarly called), and there are lesser diversions linked by the I-Ride bus.

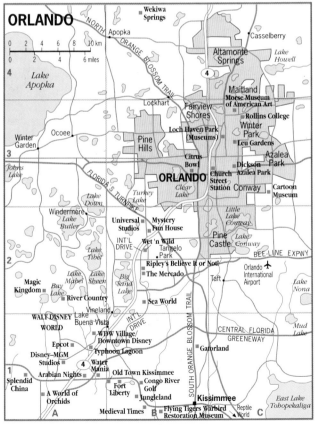

ORLANDO

0 2 4 6 8 10 km
0 2 4 6 miles

NORTH ORANGE BLOSSOM TRAIL

FLORIDA'S TURNPIKE

Wekiwa Springs
Apopka
Casselberry
Altamonte Springs
Lake Howell
Lake Apopka
Maitland
Morse Museum of American Art
Lockhart
Fairview Shores
Rollins College
Winter Park
Winter Garden
Ocoee
Pine Hills
Loch Haven Park (Museums)
Leu Gardens
Johns Lake
Citrus Bowl
Azalea Park
Dickson
ORLANDO
Church Street Station
Azalea Park
Conway
Cartoon Museum
Lake Down
Turkey Lake
Clear Lake
Windermere
Lake Butler
Universal Studios
Mystery Fun House
Little Lake Conway
Pine Castle
Lake Conway
BEE-LINE EXPWY
INT'L DRIVE
Wet 'n Wild
Tangelo Park
Lake Tibet
Ripley's Believe It or Not!
Orlando International Airport
Magic Kingdom
Lake Mabel
Lake Sheen
Big Sand Lake
The Mercado
Taft
Lake Nona
Bay Lake
River Country
Sea World
Vineland
WALT DISNEY WORLD
Lake Buena Vista
INT'L DRIVE
CENTRAL FLORIDA GREENEWAY
Mud Lake
Epcot
WDW Village/Downtown Disney
SOUTH ORANGE BLOSSOM TRAIL
Disney–MGM Studios
Typhoon Lagoon
Gatorland
Water Mania
Arabian Nights
Old Town Kissimmee
Splendid China
Fort Liberty
Congo River Golf
A World of Orchids
Jungleland
Kissimmee
East Lake Tohopekaliga
Medieval Times
Flying Tigers Warbird Restoration Museum
Reptile World

A B C

29

Opposite: *Dixieland jazz is a feature at Rosie O'Grady's, Church Street Station*

What to See in Orlando

Until recently visitors have received little encouragement to venture beyond the distinctly touristy environs of I-Drive and the major theme parks, but all that has changed with the introduction of **CultureQuest**, a shuttle bus service that ferries passengers to more than 15 of the area's top arts, sciences and historical attractions. Downtown's Church Street Station entertainment complex is on the route, as is the excellent new Orlando Science Center and adjacent historical and art museums in Loch Haven Park.

CHURCH STREET STATION ✪✪✪

This is a rather strange location for an entertainment complex, right in the middle of the downtown business district, but Church Street Station has proved a magnet for visitors and locals alike, where the good times roll 365 days a year. The setting is Victorian and works well in the famous all-singing, all-dancing showrooms which cater to a broad range of tastes. You can indulge in unfettered nostalgia, croon along to *Minnie the Moocher* and twist the night away to hits from the 1950s or fuel up with a few cocktails and hit disco heaven. The complex also boasts a choice of restaurants, an inexpensive Food Court, and a two-storey speciality shopping mall. Hour-long **balloon flights** over Central Florida, with a glass of champagne on landing, can also be arranged.

Below is a list of highlights; see also ➤ 17.

Apple Annie's Courtyard A popular meeting point and watering hole serving cocktails, fresh fruit juices and ice creams, to the accompaniment of a little blue grass music.

Cheyenne Saloon and Opera House A grand re-creation of a Wild West saloon on three levels, featuring country music Grand Ol' Opry-style, and waitstaff in cowboy kit. Top performers, terrific atmosphere and outbreaks of two-step and line dancing.

Commander Ragtime's Midway of Fun and Games On the third level of The Exchange – brash, noisy and addictive state-of-the-art video and arcade games.

✚ 29C3

✉ 129 W Church Street (I-4 to Exit 38/Anderson Street)

☎ (407) 422 2434

🕐 Daily 11–2; The Exchange shops 11–11

🍴 Lili Marlene's (££–£££); Cheyenne Saloon Barbeque Restaurant (££); Crackers Seafood Restaurant (££); Rosie O'Grady's Deli (£); Exchange Food Court (£)

♿ Good

💷 Expensive; tickets cover admission to all showrooms for the whole evening. Admission to The Exchange shops: free

❓ Check schedules for special events and the annual St Patrick's Day, Halloween and New Year's Eve Street Parties

The Exchange Some 50 speciality shops and boutiques aimed at the gift and souvenir shopper. Stock up on anything from African art to Ray Bans, lingerie from Victoria's Secret, shamrock motif braces from House of Ireland, or classy souvenir T-shirts from Destination Orlando.

Orchid Garden Dance the night away to live rock and roll classics from the 1950s to the 1990s.

Phineas Phogg's Glitter ball, light show, live music and Top 40 dance hits, in Church Street's high energy discotheque.

Rosie O'Grady's Good Time Emporium About 90 years behind the times and proud of it, Rosie's good time saloon entertainment turns the spotlight on the strumming banjos of the showboat era, can-can gals prancing down the bar top, Dixieland jazz, torch ballards, and Bourbon Street song-and-dance routines.

Wine Cellar A wine bar boasting more than 4,000 wine varieties from 150 vineyards housed in Central Florida's only wine cellar, 12-feet below Church Street.

CultureQuest Shuttle Bus

✉ Pick-ups from downtown, International Drive, Lake Buena Vista, Kissimmee

☎ Information and reservations: (407) 855 6920 or 1-800 327 5254

🕐 Wed–Sun

❓ One-off charge lasts whole day; passengers get on and off at each attraction as they please

Balloon Operators
Champagne balloon flights
☎ (407) 422 2434
Aerial Adventures of Orlando, Inc
☎ (407) 944 1070
Orange Blossom Balloons
☎ (407) 239 7677

🕇 29B1
✉ 14501 S Orange Blossom Trail
☎ (407) 855 5496 or 1-800 777 9044
🕐 Daily 8AM–dusk
🍴 Pearl's Smokehouse (£)
♿ Good
👣 Moderate

Above: *one of Gatorland's scaly residents*

GATORLAND ✪✪

Southeast of Orlando, on the border with Kissimmee, a pair of giant alligator jaws forms the entrance to this classic Florida attraction. Hundreds of captive 'gators' occupy various pens and pools. The stripey young, known as 'grunts', clamber all over each other and lie around in piles on the sunny duckboards, while the big guys, hides adorned with carpets of green algae, flash wickedly toothy grins. There are alligator shows, alligator meals (sample Gator Nuggets in Pearl's Smokehouse), and alligator products, such as wallets, boots and handbags, on sale in the gift shop. Other Gatorland residents include Florida crocodiles and caymans, native snapping and soft-shell turtles, and snake displays feature venomous rattlesnakes and cottontail moccasins.

A highlight of the park is the 2,000-foot-long marshland boardwalk edging a cypress swamp. This is a native habitat alligator breeding ground and a fabulous birdwatching spot. In spring, snowy egrets construct their twiggy nests within a few feet of passers-by, and there are great and little blue herons, pigeon-sized little green herons and dozens of other wading birds living in the water's edge rookeries.

🕇 29C3
✉ 1920 N Forest Avenue
☎ (407) 246 2620
🕐 Daily 9–5 except Christmas Day. Leu House tours Tue–Sat 10–3:30, Sun–Mon 1–3:30
♿ Good
👣 Moderate
↔ Orange County Historical Museum, Orlando Museum of Art, Orlando Science Center (▶ 34–5)

LEU GARDENS ✪✪✪

Sloping gently down to the shores of Lake Rowena, these lovely 50-acre formal gardens provide a soothing escape from the hustle and bustle. They were originally laid out by local businessman Harry P Leu and his wife, who purchased the property in 1936, and lived in historic Leu House, a much-enlarged old pioneer home in the middle of the gardens.

Near the entrance, the lush Ravine Garden leads down to a boardwalk and a gazebo which overlooks the lake. Coots and ducks potter about in the lake's waters and the occasional wild alligator lurks here. To the west of the property, mature southern magnolias and spreading live oaks shade the camellia woods, which can be seen at their best during the October to March flowering season. The Leus planted more than 2,000 camellia specimens here, and their collection is considered to be one of the finest in the eastern US.

The floral centerpiece is the Rose Garden, a popular setting for open-air weddings among the 1,000 scented rose bushes. Close by, Leu House is open for regular tours. In the far corner of the gardens, the Display Greenhouse is a riot of hothouse orchids, tropical gingers, anthuriums, heliconias and ferns.

LOCH HAVEN PARK ✪
This lakeside park makes a pleasant and useful picnic stop for visitors who are on their way to the Orlando museums (➤ 34–5).

Below: *Mystery Fun House – located just across from Universal Studios*

✚ 29B3
✉ Princeton Street (1 mile east of I-4/Exit 43)
🕐 Open site
💷 Free

MYSTERY FUN HOUSE ✪
Once a big hit, the Fun House is now outclassed by the slick presentation and sophisticated rides at the top end of the theme park market. However, undemanding children may be reasonably entertained by the mirror maze, wobbly floors, dusty Egyptian mummies and a blind grope through the catacombs. Connoisseurs of the truly tacky will appreciate the wallet-lightening encounter with a computerized 'gypsy palm-reading' machine and a 15-minute film show in The Wizard's Theater of Horror, featuring a mish-mash of clips from famous horror movies. Also mini-golf, arcade and laser games.

✚ 29B2
✉ 5767 Major Boulevard (I-4/Exit 30-B)
☎ (407) 351 3355
🕐 Daily 10AM–late
🍴 Cafeteria and ice cream parlour (£)
♿ Few
💷 Moderate
↔ Universal Studios (➤ 40–2)

✚ 29C3
✉ Loch Haven Park, E
Princeton Street (I-4/Exit
43)
☎ (407) 897 6350
⊘ Mon–Sat 9–5, Sun 12–5
♿ Good
👆 Cheap
↔ Leu Gardens (➤ 32),
Orlando Museum of Art,
Orlando Science Center
(see below)

ORANGE COUNTY HISTORICAL MUSEUM ✪

An interesting detour for amateur historians who would like to find out a little more about Orlando and Central Florida pre-Mouse. Some of the most eye-catching exhibits here are the turn-of-the-century photographs of downtown Orlando and roughneck Cracker cowmen (so-called either because they cracked whips or because they cracked corn to make grits, the old-time rural South's staple diet). There is a re-creation of a pioneer kitchen and a Victorian parlour, plus an exhaustive history of the region's citrus industry upstairs.

Across the yard, the 1926 red brick Fire Station No 3 houses a museum of fire-fighting. This is a treasure trove of antique kit and memorabilia. Pride of place goes to the gleaming 1911 steam-powered fire engine complete with burnished nickel fittings and goldleaf decoration.

Right: *Orlando
Museum of Art
has a renowned
pre-Columbian
collection*
Opposite: *Vincent
van Gogh – a self-
portrait created
from 10,000
picture postcards
at Ripley's
Believe It or Not!*

✚ 29C3
✉ Loch Haven
Park, E
Princeton Street
(I-4/Exit 43)
☎ (407) 896 4231
⊘ Tue–Sat 9–5,
Sun 12–5.
Closed Mon
♿ Good
👆 Moderate
↔ Leu Gardens (➤ 32),
Orange County Historical
Museum (see above),
Orlando Science Center
(see below)

ORLANDO MUSEUM OF ART ✪

After recent renovations the museum frequently hosts visiting art shows and events, so check out current exhibition schedules. If the permanent collections are on show, visitors will be rewarded with a notable collection of pre-Columbian art – some 250 pieces dating from around 1200 BC to AD 1500 – plus works by leading 19th- to 20th-century American artists and African art exhibits.

ORLANDO SCIENCE CENTER ✪✪

Topped by a distinctive silver observatory dome, Orlando's impressive new Science Center opened its doors in 1997. The exhibits are laid out over four levels and include dozens of interactive displays and hands-on educational games designed to appeal to children of all ages – and not a few adults as well.

On ground level, the NatureWorks Florida habitat section combines models and living exhibits such as turtles, baby alligators and a reef tank, and there is the excellent KidsTown early learning area for 8s and under. On Levels 2, 3 and 4, more elaborate and sophisticated exhibits tackle the basics of physics, mathematics, applied technologies and human biology in comprehensible and entertaining style. Movie moguls should definitely see the TechWorks exhibit on Level 4, which explores the behind-the-scenes tricks of the movie trade.

In addition, there are daily science-orientated shows in the Darden Adventure Theater and the Digistar Planetarium, and large format film presentations in the CineDome, which boasts a massive 8,000 square-foot IMAX screen. On Friday and Saturday nights, while the CineDome features 3-D laser light shows, the Observatory welcomes visitors for an evening's star-gazing.

✚ 29C3
✉ 777 E Princeton Street (I-4/Exit 43)
☎ (407) 514 2000 or 1-800 672 4386
🕐 Mon–Thu 9–5, Fri–Sat 9–9, Sun 12–5. Closed Thanksgiving and Christmas
🍴 OSC Cafe (£)
♿ Very good
💰 Moderate
↔ Leu Gardens (➤ 32), Orange County Historical Museum, Orlando Museum of Art (see above)

RIPLEY'S BELIEVE IT OR NOT! MUSEUM ✪

A whacky, lop-sided building tipping down an imaginary sinkhole, a hologram greeting from the long-dead Robert L Ripley and hundreds of curious, eccentric and downright bizarre exhibits add up to a fairly unbelievable attraction. Robert Ripley was a connoisseur of oddities. Travelling extensively in the 1920s and 1930s, he amassed enough material to stock more than a dozen 'museums' of this type worldwide. Typical exhibits include a Mona Lisa made from 1,426 squares of toast and a three-quarter scale model of a 1907 Rolls Royce Silver Ghost made out of 1,016,711 matchsticks and 63 pints of glue.

✚ 29B2
✉ 8201 International Drive
☎ (407) 345 0501 or 1-800 998 4418
🕐 Daily 9AM–11PM
♿ Good
🚌 I-Ride, Lynx #42
💰 Moderate

In the Know

If you only have a short time to visit Orlando, or would like to get a flavour of the region, here are some ideas:

10
Ways To Be A Local

Dress comfortably and coolly. Floridians are also casual dressers and jackets and ties for men are rarely required.

Friday night is party night, when locals and visitors rub shoulders at downtown's Church Street Station entertainment complex (➤ 30–1).

Gator wrestling is best left to the professionals. Instead, watch a demonstration at Gatorland (➤ 32).

Go fishing – this is how the locals relax, leaving the theme parks to visitors.

'Have a nice day' is not just an automatic platitude in Orlando: people really mean it.

Sample grits, the breakfast porridge of the Southern US, made from roughly ground boiled corn mixed with butter.

Tipping is a way of life here, not just in bars and restaurants, but for just about any kind of service from valet parking to shuttle bus drivers.

Tolls are payable on the Bee Line Expressway and Florida Turnpike, so keep some small change in the car.

Turn right on red at traffic lights in Florida unless a stop sign dictates otherwise – but look out for other road-users and pedestrians.

Western wear is high fashion during Kissimmee's famous rodeo events. Snap up a pair of alligator-skin boots (➤ 107).

10
Good Places To Cool Off

Blizzard Beach (➤ 88).
Blue Spring (➤ 51).
Canaveral National Seashore offers 30 miles of unspoilt seashore and beaches stretching north of the Kennedy Space Center (➤ 58).
Cocoa Beach is one of Florida's famous 'party' beaches on the Atlantic Coast, an hour's drive down the Bee Line Expressway/SR528.
River Country (➤ 90).
Tanganyika Tidal Wave at Busch Gardens (➤ 50).
Typhoon Lagoon (➤ 90).
Water Mania (➤ 66).
Wekiwa Springs (➤ 64).
Wet 'n' Wild (➤ 43).

10
Best Theme Park Restaurants

To make advance reservations, contact Guest Relations on entering the park.
Aloha Polynesian Luau
✉ Sea World, Orlando
☎ (407) 351 3600 or 1-800 227 8048. Dinner-only South Seas feast and entertainment (call ahead

'Have a nice day'

to make reservations).
Brown Derby ✉ Disney-MGM Studios, Walt Disney World ☎ (407) 939 3463. Cool and clubby replica of Hollywood moguls' meeting place. Pasta, steaks, Cobb salad.
Buccaneer Smokehouse ✉ Sea World, Orlando ☎ (407) 351 3600. Mesquite-grilled barbecued ribs, chicken and beef.
Chefs de France ✉ Epcot Center, Walt Disney World ☎ (407) 939 3463. Elegant Disney outpost for French *nouvelle cuisine*.
Coral Reef ✉ Epcot Center, Walt Disney World ☎ (407) 939 3463. First-class seafood and a stunning view of the coral reef exhibition.
Crown Colony ✉ Busch Gardens, Tampa ☎ (813) 987 5600. Family restaurant overlooking the animals of the Serengeti Plain exhibit. Chicken dinners, fresh seafood, sandwiches.
Hard Rock Café ✉ Universal Studios, Orlando ☎ (407) 351 7625. Big fun, big name rock memorabilia and big burgers.
Hong Kong Seafood Restaurant ✉ Splendid China, Kissimmee ☎ (407) 397 8800. Chinese cuisine and familiar favourites, from Cantonese crispy shrimp to Hong Kong beef filet.
Liberty Tree Tavern ✉ Magic Kingdom, Walt Disney World ☎ (407) 939 3463. All-American home-style cooking in a re-created colonial inn. Turkey dinners, Cape Cod pasta, pot roast.
Lombard's Landing ✉ Universal Studios, Orlando ☎ (407) 224 6400. Seafood specialities, pasta and

steaks, plus waterfront dining in the re-created San Francisco district.

10

Top Golf Courses

Arnold Palmer's Bay Hill Club ✉ 9000 Bay Hill Boulevard, Orlando ☎ (407) 876 8008.
Black Bear Golf Club ✉ 24505 Calusa Boulevard, Eustis ☎ (352) 357 4732 or 1-800 423 2718.
Falcon's Fire Golf Club ✉ 3200 Seralago Boulevard, Kissimmee ☎ (407) 239 5445.
Grand Cypress ✉ Hyatt Regency Grand Cypress, One Grand Cypress Boulevard, Orlando ☎ (407) 239 1234.
Lake Buena Vista Course ✉ Walt Disney World ☎ (407) 824 2270.
Metro West Country Club ✉ 2100 S Hiawassee Road, Orlando ☎ (407) 299 8800.
Mission Inn Golf & Tennis Resort ✉ 10400 CR48, Howey-in-the-Hills ☎ (352) 324 3101 or 1-800 874 9053.
Orange Lake Resort & Country Club ✉ 8505 W Irlo Bronson Memorial Highway/US192, Kissimmee ☎ (407) 239 0000 or 1-800 877 6522.
Palm Course ✉ Walt Disney World ☎ (407) 824 2270.
Timacuan Golf & Country Club ✉ 550 Timacuan Boulevard, Lake Mary ☎ (407) 321 0014.

10

Free Attractions

Albin Polasek Galleries ✉ 633 Osceola Avenue, Winter Park ☎ (407) 647 6294. Works from the Czech-American sculptor

in galleries and gardens.
Cornell Fine Arts Museum ✉ Rollins College, Winter Park ☎ (407) 646 2526. Old Masters and contemporary fine arts (➤ 67).
Florida Audubon Society ✉ 1101 Audubon Way, Maitland ☎ (407) 539 5700. Aviaries housing birds of prey, including eagles, owls and hawks.
Historic Waterhouse Residence and Carpentry Shop Museums ✉ 820 Lake Lily Drive, Maitland ☎ (407) 644 2451. Restored 1884 residence and carpentry shop.
Kennedy Space Center ✉ SR405, Merritt Island ☎ (407) 452 2121 or 1-800 572 4636. Admission to the visitor centre is free (➤ 20, 59).
Lake Eola Park ✉ Eola Drive, Orlando ☎ (407) 246 2827. Downtown's lakeside park with picnicking areas, children's playground and boat rentals.
Lakeridge Winery & Vineyards ✉ 19239 N US27, Clermont ☎ (352) 394 8627 or 1-800 768 9463. Guided tours and tastings.
Maitland Art Center ✉ 231 W Packwood Avenue, Maitland ☎ (407) 539 2181. Art exhibits and classes in a 1930s artists' colony decorated with Aztec-Mayan carvings.
Maitland Historical Museum & Telephone Museum ✉ 221 W Packwood Avenue, Maitland ☎ (407) 644 1364. Artefacts, photos and memorabilia.
Zora Neale Hurston National Museum of Fine Arts ✉ 227 E Kennedy Boulevard, Eatonville ☎ (407) 647 3307. Exhibits by artists of African descent in Zora Neale Hurston's (➤ 14) home town.

SEA WORLD ✪✪✪

Sea World's well-balanced combination of sights and shows is a proven winner. Unlike some parks, where the shows are incidental to the main action, here they are an intrinsic ingredient, and the rest of the attractions can be fitted in as visitors make their way around the various show stadiums.

From spring 1998, visitors can go on a new, hair-raising Journey to Atlantis, combining a high-speed water ride with state-of-the-art special effects. Passengers board rickety Greek fishing boats for a sightseeing trip to the newly risen city of Atlantis which goes horribly wrong as they are swept off into the mysterious and spooky depths of the Sirens' Lair.

Sunset reveals another side of Sea World, with nightly laser and fireworks displays over the Bayside Stadium. Another popular event is the **Aloha Polynesian Luau Buffet and South Seas Musical Revue** .

Below is a list of highlights; see also ► 21.

Cydesdale Hamlet Theme park owners and brewers Anheuser-Busch maintain a pristine stable area for their giant Scottish Clydesdale draft horses. The Anheuser-Busch Hospitality Center is here, too, and beer-lovers can sign up for classes at the Beer School.

Key West at Sea World A new Florida Keys themed area, with a tropical atmosphere and street performers. The centerpiece is two-acre Dolphin Cove, a lagoon habitat for Atlantic bottlenose dolphins adjacent to the Whale & Dolphin Stadium. Rescued turtles bask on the rocks of Turtle Point, visitors can feed and pet captive stingrays in the Stingray Lagoon, and there are nightly festivities in Sunset Square.

Manatees: The Last Generation? Distant aquatic relative of the elephant, the manatee is now a seriously endangered species. There may be fewer than 2,000 of these giant Florida sea cows left in the wild. All the manatees in this Sea World exhibit are rescued and will be returned to the wild if possible.

Pacific Point Preserve California sea lions, harbour seals and South American fur seals occupy this rocky northern Pacific coast re-creation, complete with wave machine. On sunny days the animals float around on their backs with flippers in the air to regulate body temperature.

Penguin Encounter Hundreds of Antarctic penguins and their Arctic cousins, the alcids (better known as puffins and mures), inhabit these icy confines. Behind the glass, the air is kept at a constant 34°F and a snow machine dusts the polar scene.

Shamu's Happy Harbor Play area for small children with climbing apparatus, radio-controlled boats, a sandpit and face-painting activities.

Terrors of the Deep Spooky music and eerie lighting accompany these aquariums full of lurking moray eels, 28mph barracudas and highly toxic puffer fish. Ride the perspex tunnel through the 660,000-gallon shark tank, also home to the small-toothed swordfish, with his chainsaw-like nose blade used to slash through schools of fish.

Wild Arctic A simulated helicopter ride transports visitors to an Arctic base station for close encounters with polar bears, beluga whales and walruses. However, the icy habitats are distinctly cramped for these large animals.

Below: a *fascinating underwater exhibit provides a clear view of all the drama and action of the sea*
Inset: *killer whales on form at Sea World*

Souvenir T-shirt

🕂 29B2

✉ 1000 Universal Studios
Plaza, Orlando (I-4/Exit 29
or 30-B)

☎ (407) 363 8000

🕐 Daily from 9AM; closing
times vary

🍴 17 cafés, burger bars, ice
cream parlours (£), and
restaurants including
Lombard's Landing (££);
Hard Rock Café (££);
Louie's Italian Restaurant
(£–££)

♿ Very good

✋ Very expensive.
Reduced-price Vacation
Value Passes provide
unlimited access to
Orlando's Sea World,
Universal Studios, and
Wet 'n' Wild, and Busch
Gardens, Tampa over
five- or seven-day
periods. Available from
the parks

↔ Wet 'n' Wild (➤ 43)

UNIVERSAL STUDIOS   ✪✪✪

It would be a mistake to assume that if you have done
Walt Disney World's Disney-MGM Studios (➤ 70–5) you
should skip Universal. The Universal theme park
experience is more ride-orientated than its Disney rival and
the attractive layout is a plus, particularly the central lagoon
with its waterfront restaurants and snack bars.

The most popular shows on the Universal lot include
the Wild, Wild, Wild West Stunt Show; Beetlejuice's
Graveyard Revue; the 1950s Hollywood Hi-Tones at Mel's
Diner, and Blues Brothers soul-style entertainment. After
dark do not miss the powerboats and pyrotechnics of the
Dynamite Nights Stuntacular on the lagoon.

Fans of the inimitably dizzy Lucille Ball will enjoy Lucy:
A Tribute, with costumes, props, home movies and
personal letters, plus interactive video games to test your
'Lucy IQ'.

The Gory, Gruesome & Grotesque Horror Make-
Up Show reveals tricks of the horror movie trade, including
the transformation of man to beast in An *American
Werewolf in London*, and Linda Blair's swivelling head in
The Exorcist.

Next door to Barney's Theater, which hosts regular
performances of the dinosaur show A Day in the Park with
Barney, the Barney's Backyard indoor play area is a handy
retreat for small children on a hot day, with slides, tree
houses, soft building blocks and a mini maze in air-condi-
tioned comfort.

Below is a list of highlights; see also ➤ 26.

Alfred Hitchcock: The Art of Making Movies An educational behind-the-scenes homage to the master of
Hollywood suspense, with screen presentations by
Hitchcock himself. Sample a hair-raising 3-D snippet from
The Birds , re-create the famous *Psycho* shower scene,
and get a close look at some of the director's most
effective film techniques in the Hitchcock Interactive Area.
Animal Actors Stage An exotic jungle temple setting for
trained animal antics by the likes of Olly the stunt chimp
and assorted other animals, most rescued from shelters.

Back to the Future...The Ride One of the most ambitious theme park rides ever created, this four-minute, 21-million jigowatt spin in Doc Brown's time-travelling DeLorean is a must, with its wild simulator action and 70mm IMAX screens.

Earthquake – The Big One It is a short step off the San Francisco street set to this subway journey from hell. Experience an 8.3 on the Richter Scale, as portrayed in the classic 1974 disaster movie *Earthquake*. Witness 45,000-pound pillars tumbling to the ground, 65,000 gallons of water swirling through the underground station, and learn the tricks of the special effects trade.

Top: *Earthquake – The Big One*
Above: *outside Mel's Drive-In, from* American Graffiti

ET Adventure A gentle ride over 3,340 miniature buildings aboard flying bicycles with ET in a basket on the front handlebars. A ride that appeals to younger children.

Fievel's Playland Outsize props lend a mouse's eye view to this popular adventure playground with a mini assault course laid out around a 1,000-gallon cowboy hat, harmonica-styled slide and giant tea set. Adults can also join in for a ride down the twisting 200-foot water slide.

Funtastic World of Hanna-Barbera A cast of cartoon favourites from the splendid animation team of Bill Hanna and Joe Barbera feature in this entertaining simulator ride. After the ride you can play on the animation computers in the Interactive Area.

41

Hercules and Xena Top-rated American TV shows *Hercules: The Legendary Journeys* and *Xena: Warrior Princess*, team up for this action-packed experience featuring state-of-the-art effects and live action stunt performers. Swashbuckling audience volunteers join in some of the fight scenes.

Jaws Set among the seaside architecture and artfully arranged lobster pots of a re-created fishing village, Captain Jake's Amity Boat Tours embark for a wholly expected watery encounter with the glistening jaws of Universal's famous 32-foot, three-ton mechanical great white shark. The steel-and-fibreglass shark moves at speeds of up to 20 feet per second, with a thrust power equal to a 727 jet engine. Passengers still love it, and this is a particularly attractive corner of the park.

Kongfrontation Hop aboard a New York City Transit tram bound for Roosevelt Island and experience the Kongfrontation of a lifetime as a six-ton, four-storey-high Kong creates havoc in downtown Manhattan. The aerial tram car swings perilously above the deserted streets, braving crashing masonry and fire balls, as well as the alarmingly banana-breathed ape. Splendidly kitsch.

Nickelodeon Studios World Headquarters The nerve centre for America's top kid-tested and kid-approved children's television network. The soundstage tour is a bit long-winded, though the visit to the Gak Kitchen, where sublimely oozy, gloppy dollops of top-quality slime and goo are tested on willing young human guinea pigs, is a favourite stop. Then it is on to the Game Lab for some audience participation testing new games.

Terminator 2: 3-D Battle Across Time The world's first 3-D virtual adventure, 'T2:3-D' (to aficionados) reunited the *Terminator 2* team to produce the most expensive film, frame for frame, ever made: $24 million for 12 minutes. The audience is transported into an apocalyptic world, showered with 3-D flying debris and whirlygig mini-hunter pocket gunships, and menaced by the flexi-steel pincers of the re-generating T-1,000,000. Fantastic effects: not to be missed, however long the queue.

Twister Newly translated from the blockbuster movie, this multi-million dollar tornado encounter is not for the faint-hearted. Brave a five-storey-high cyclone, complete with torrential rain and howling winds.

Below: *Wet 'n' Wild claims more rides than any other water park in Florida*

WET 'N' WILD ✪✪

The hottest way to cool off on International Drive, this 25-acre landmark water park offers dozens of thrills and spills, a scaled-down Kid's Park pool area and sunbathing decks. The latest heart-stopper is the four-person Fuji Flyer, an in-line water toboggan ride inspired by death-defying bobsled runs on Mount Fuji, Japan. Old favourites include the 500-foot twisting descent of the Black Hole, in total darkness; the seven-storey Bomb Bay drop, and Der Stuka, one of the highest, fastest waterslides in the world. Meanwhile, family-sized inflatables tackle The Surge and Bubba Tub, or drift down Lazy River on a giant inner tube.

🔒 29B2
✉ 6200 International Drive (I-4/Exit 30-A)
☎ (407) 351 1800 or 1-800 992 9453
🕐 Daily, variable hours from 9am in summer (10AM winter); call for schedules
🍴 Concessions (£)
🚌 I-Ride, Lynx #42
♿ Few
💲 Expensive. Reduced-price Vacation Value Passes provide unlimited access to Orlando's Sea World, Universal Studios, and Wet 'n' Wild, and Busch Gardens, Tampa over five- or seven-day periods. Available from the parks
↔ Universal Studios (➤ 26, 40–3)

43

Quality Inn

GREAT SERVICE

KEY W. KOOLS

SEAFOOD · STEAK

BREAKFAST

Around Orlando

An all-but-invisible line divides Greater Orlando from neighbouring Kissimmee. Walt Disney World has transformed the former cattle town, bringing a welter of budget hotels and low-priced attractions along US192. Kissimmee is no beauty, but it is a useful family resort area, where the prices are fair and the entertainment is on tap, attracting around 10 million annual overnight visitors.

Beyond Orlando and Kissimmee, Central Florida offers a wide choice of attractive day trips. Fast highways lead to top sight-seeing destinations such as the Kennedy Space Center on the Atlantic coast and Tampa's Busch Gardens in little more than an hour. Equally accessible are the horticultural highlights of Cypress Gardens and Bok Tower Gardens, near Winter Haven, and there are unspoilt state park preserves where hiking trails, canoe runs and wildlife-spotting provide the perfect antidote to the hurly-burly of the theme parks.

＊

*'Central Florida – a
study in reality
suspension, brought to
your imagination by the
nation's finest fantasy
makers.'*

FLORIDA TOURIST BOARD

Colourful blooms at A World of Orchids

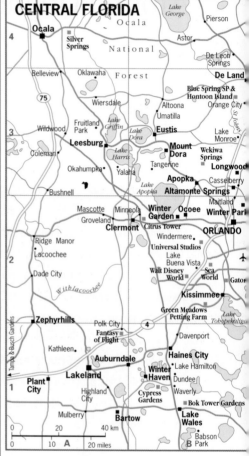

CENTRAL FLORIDA

4 — Ocala · Silver Springs · Ocala · Lake George · Pierson · Astor · De Leon Springs · De Land

Belleview · Oklawaha · National Forest · Blue Spring SP & Hontoon Island · Orange City · De Land

75 · Wiersdale · Altoona · Umatilla · Lake Monroe

3 — Wildwood · Fruitland Park · Lake Griffin · Lake Dora · Eustis · Wekiwa Springs · Longwood

Leesburg · Lake Harris · Mount Dora · Tangerine · Casselberry

Coleman · Okahumpka · Yalaha · Apopka · Maitland

Bushnell · Lake Apopka · Altamonte Springs · Winter Park

Mascotte · Minneola · Winter Garden · Ocoee · ORLANDO

Groveland · Clermont · Citrus Tower · Windermere

Ridge Manor · Universal Studios · Lake Buena Vista

2 — Lacoochee · Walt Disney World · Sea World · Gator

Dade City · Withlacoochee · Kissimmee

Zephyrhills · Polk City · Green Meadows Petting Farm · Lake Tohopekaliga

Fantasy of Flight · Davenport

Kathleen · Auburndale · Haines City · Lake Hamilton

Tampa & Busch Gardens · Plant City · Lakeland · Winter Haven · Dundee · Waverly

1 — Highland City · Cypress Gardens · Bok Tower Gardens

Mulberry · Bartow · Lake Wales · Babson Park

0 — 20 — 40 km
0 — 10 — A — 20 miles — B

What to See Around Orlando

A WORLD OF ORCHIDS

Harboured in a half-acre, climate-controlled greenhouse jungle, the world's largest permanent indoor display of flowering orchids is quite a sight. There are more than 2,000 orchid species on view and they come in an incredible array of colours, shapes, sizes and delicate scents, set against a lush backdrop of exuberant tropical foliage, gingers, palms and dramatic bird-of-paradise flowers. It is worth taking one of the daily guided tours (11 and 3; also 1 on weekends). Outside, native Floridian orchids can be seen from the short boardwalk nature trail; there is a catfish angling pool and pigeon displays.

29A1
2501 Old Lake Wilson Road/CR-545 (NM 5.5), Kissimmee
(407) 396 1887
Daily 9:30–5:30. Closed New Year's Day, 4 July, Thanksgiving, Christmas Day
Few
Moderate
Splendid China (► 23, 65)

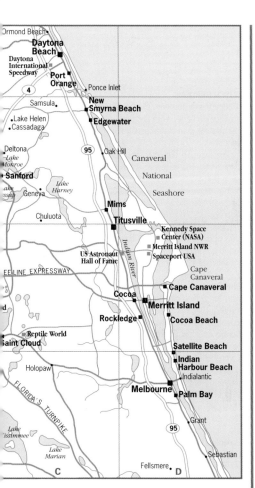

Elegant Bok Tower, on the Florida peninsula's highest point, Iron Mountain

BOK TOWER GARDENS

A short drive from the more overt charms of Cypress Gardens, these lovely woodland gardens are a real haven of peace and quiet. Dutch philanthropist Edward W Bok created the gardens in the 1920s and added the coquina rock and marble bell tower, with its world-class carillon. The tower is perched on top of Iron Mountain, the highest point on the Florida peninsula, at a modest 298 feet above sea level, and the gently sloping 157-acre gardens contain thousands of flowering azaleas, camellias and magnolias beneath a canopy of oaks, palms and pines. There are daily carillon recitals and tours of the elegant 1930s Mediterranean Revival-style Pinewood House and Gardens in the grounds on certain days.

46B1

CR17-A (off Alt. 27, 3 miles north of Lake Wales)

(941) 676 9412

Daily 8–5

Garden Restaurant (£)

Good

Inexpensive

Cypress Gardens (► 18, 52), Lake Wales (► 61)

Daily carillon recitals at 3PM; concerts for special events.

✚ 46A1

✉ Busch Boulevard, Tampa
(75 miles west of Orlando
via I-4 West and I-75
North to Fowler
Avenue/Exit 54)

☎ (813) 987 5082

🕐 Daily 9:30–6 (extended
summer and hols)

🍴 Refreshment stops
throughout park, plus:
Zagora Café (Morocco);
Das Festhaus (Timbuktu);
Anheuser-Busch
Hospitality Center and
Crown Colony Restaurant
(Crown Colony); Vivi
Storehouse Restaurant
(Congo); Stanleyville
Smokehouse
(Stanleyville); Hospitality
House (Bird Gardens)
(£–££)

♿ Very good

💲 Very expensive.
Reduced-price Vacation
Value Passes provide
unlimited access to
Orlando's Sea World,
Universal Studios, and
Wet 'n' Wild, and Busch
Gardens, Tampa over
five- or seven-day
periods. Available from
the parks

❓ Check daily schedules for
show times

BUSCH GARDENS

A popular side trip from Orlando, Busch Gardens provides a full day's family entertainment in a sprawling, African-inspired zoo-cum-theme park complex on the outskirts of Tampa.

There are 10 themed areas, each offering a choice of attractions. The excellent water rides are very wet, and rainproof capes are on sale, but few sunbaked visitors bother. However, it is a good idea to bring a change of clothes and avoid an uncomfortably soggy journey back to Orlando.

Opposite the Busch Gardens complex, Anheuser-Busch also operate a popular 36-acre water park, Adventure Island (summer only).

Below is a list of highlights; see also ➤ 16.

Bird Gardens Flamingos, ducks, ibis and koi fish do battle with screeching gulls for titbits in the leafy lagoon areas of the Bird Gardens. There is a walk-though aviary, an eagle exhibit, bird shows, and captive koala bears.

Congo An action-packed area at the northern extent of the park, the Congo's attractions include the hair-raising Kumba roller coaster. The slightly less dramatic Python still manages two 360° loops and a 70-foot plunge. A drenching is guaranteed on the Congo River Rapids, and onlookers can man the Waterblasters on the bridge (25c a shot). The Ubanga-Banga Bumper Cars are located here, too; the Transveldt Railway Train stops at the station; and the park's magnificent Bengal tigers are incarcerated on undersized Claw Island.

Crown Colony Here you can eat at the park's only full-service dining room, the Crown Colony Restaurant, look in on the Anheuser-Busch brewery's ceremonial draft horses, and take a ride on Questor, a stomach-churning simulator ride.

Egypt Ruined columns, giant carved figures and hiero-glyphics provide the setting for a journey into Tut's Tomb, a walk-through tour of a replica pyramid tomb as discovered by the archaeologist Howard Carter in the 1920s. The contemporary news reel footage is fun, but the jewels look a little pasty. The big ride here is the 3,983-foot-long, 150-foot-high Montu roller coaster, featuring the world's largest inverted coaster loop at 104 feet. The Transveldt Railway Train travels across the Serengeti Plain.

Land of the Dragons A well-designed adventure playground for small children, with a friendly dragon theme. The three-storey Dragon's Nest treehouse is lavishly equipped with stairs and ropeways, and there are

Above: *the Tanganyika Tidal Wave*
Left: *beyond Orlando, Busch Gardens is the most visited theme park in Florida*

slides, a sandpit, a carousel, watery activities and a children's theatre. The Living Dragons display features monitor lizards, Komodo dragons from Indonesia and giant iguanas.

Morocco At the entrance to the park, Morocco features attractive Moorish-style architecture and a clutch of souk-like stores selling North African craft items. Ice shows are held at the Moroccan Palace Theater and other diversions scheduled in the Marrakesh Theater and Tangiers Theater.

*Enjoying a jumbo ride at
Busch Gardens*

Serengeti Plain transport

 Elevated monorail (round-
trip): Crown Colony. Sky
Ride cable car: Crown
Colony, Stanleyville.
Transveldt Railway Train:
Egypt, Congo,
Stanleyville

Nairobi First stop is Myombe Reserve: The Great Ape
Domain, where the park's western lowland gorillas and
chimpanzees nit-pick, snooze and occasionally stir
themselves to get a better look at the humans. There are
vampire bats, reptiles and snakes in Curiousity Caverns;
baby birds and other residents in the Animal Nursery; a
petting zoo, giant tortoises and elephants.

Serengeti Plain A 60-acre grassland enclosure
reminiscent of the African veldt, inhabited by antelopes,
giraffes, lions, rhinos and zebras. The park's newest
attraction, Edge of Africa, promises a safari experience
with close-up views of the animals, via a series of imagina-
tively designed enclosures, complete with a backing track
of animal sounds and a range of evocative African smells
running the olfactory gamut from camp fire to termite
mound. Inspect an abandoned Masai village overrun by
lions and hyenas, hippos wallowing in a riverine habitat,
baboons, crocodiles and meerkats.

Stanleyville Just the place to cool off with two great
water rides: Tanganyika Tidal Wave (which soaks
onlookers as well as passengers); and Stanley Falls Log
Flume. There are reptile encounters at Snakes and More;
the warthog and orangutan habitats; and a black spider
monkey colony cavorting behind the fragrant and colourful
Orchid Canyon.

Timbuktu At the heart of the park, Timbuktu's diversions
include regular shows in the Dolphin Theater, the German-
themed Festhaus; thrills aboard the Scorpion roller coaster
and other fairground attractions, and arcade games.

A Tour Around Blue Spring State Park

One of the prettiest state parks in Central Florida, Blue Spring is also famous for its winter season manatee population. The manatees usually visit between November and March, but the park is a great day out all year round, offering walking, boating and swimming opportunites, and it is a good place to enjoy a picnic (see panel, ➤ 96).

From Orlando, take I-4 east (direction Daytona) to Exit 52. Follow US17–92 north to Orange City. Blue Spring State Park is signposted off to the left at the junction with W French Avenue.

A Jungle Cruise is an excellent way to enjoy Silver Springs' wildlife

Lying along the wooded banks of the St Johns River, Florida's longest natural waterway, the park's namesake artesian spring is one of the largest in the US producing around 100 million gallons of water a day. It really is blue, too. The turquoise pool at the spring head is a popular swimming hole for snorkelling, scuba-diving or just splashing around to cool off in the heat of the day.

During winter the warm spring waters, which gush forth at a constant 72°F, attract manatees from the cooler waters of the St Johns. From the waterside boardwalk there is a bird's eye view of the manatees, and dozens of different fish and turtles swimming in the spring run; numerous waterbirds also congregate here. Canoes are available for rental and there are boat trips down the St Johns to nearby Hontoon Island State Park.

Follow the walking trail which starts near the Steamboat-era Thursby House.

Thursby House itself is perched on top of an ancient shell mound, left by Timucuan Indians. The trail leads through sand pine scrub, marshland and flatwood areas of the park.

Return to Orange City and take US17–92/I–4 back to Orlando.

Distance
60 miles round trip

Time
A 45-minute drive from Orlando. Allow at least 2 hours in the park

Start/end point
Orlando
✚ 46B2

Destination
Blue Spring State Park
✚ 46B3
✉ 2100 W French Avenue, Orange City
☎ (904) 775 3663
🕐 Daily 8AM–sunset
💲 Inexpensive

Lunch
Snack concessions and cold drinks available in the park

29B1

✉ 4777 W Irlo Bronson Highway/US192 (NM 12), Kissimmee; also at 6312 International Drive, Orlando

☎ (407) 396 6900

🕐 Daily 10AM–late

🚻 Few

💲 Moderate

↔ Flying Tigers Warbird Restoration Museum (➤ 53), Jungleland (➤ 55)

46B1

✉ State Road 540 W, 4 miles east of Winter Haven (off US27, 22 miles south of I-4)

☎ (941) 324 2111 or 1-800 282 2123

🕐 Daily 9–5:30 (extended summer and hols)

Southern belles, in their antebellum dresses, adorn the grounds at Cypress Gardens

CONGO RIVER GOLF ✪

There is a choice of routes around this nifty mini-golf course and players are challenged to follow in the footsteps of 19th-century African explorers Henry Stanley and Dr David Livingstone. The obstacles are somewhat less dramatic and debilitating than those encountered by our heroes (there are no tsetse flies in Kissimmee), but the tropical layout is well provided with waterfalls, streams and mountainous boulders beneath the swaying palm trees. For those 'too pooped to putt', there are paddle boats and a games arcade. At the second location on International Drive, go-karts add to the fun.

CYPRESS GARDENS ✪✪✪

Florida's most sedate theme park, as well as its oldest, Cypress Gardens has until recently rather rested on its laurels, or rather its huge and colourful floral displays. The Botanical Gardens are still a treat, and there are flower festivals and impressive shows of massed blooms in the formal gardens throughout the year.

However, families can now enjoy visiting the Wings of Wonder butterfly conservatory, where it is fun to spot the hidden iguanas, turtles and tiny Asian doves. Birds of prey and reptile discovery shows are part of the new Nature's Way animal habitat exhibit; and daily entertainment programmes feature concerts, shows, water-skiing spectaculars and night-time laser light shows.

See also ➤ 18.

FANTASY OF FLIGHT ✪✪✪

Aviation historian, aerobatic pilot, designer and vintage aircraft restorer Kermit Weeks' second Florida air museum (the original is in Miami) showcases exhibits from Weeks' private aircraft collection alongside history displays and entertaining simulator rides.

Aviation buffs will find plenty to enjoy here down among the World War I fighters, 1920s barnstormers, Spitfires, Wildcats and Dauntless dive bombers from World War II – and even a battered Japanese Zero fighter, rescued from the treetops of New Guinea in the early 1990s. Aviation oddities are featured too, such as the Roadair flying automobile with retractable wings for highway driving, and an accurate replica of Charles A Lindbergh's *Spirit of St Louis*, which made the first trans-atlantic flight in 1927.

See also ➤ 19.

🕇 46A1
✉ SR-559, Polk City (I-4 West to Exit 21)
☎ (941) 984 3500
🕐 Daily 9–5 (extended summer and hols)

The Flying Tigers Warbird Restoration Museum preserves World War II airplanes in pristine flying condition

FLYING TIGERS WARBIRD RESTORATION MUSEUM ✪

From the slick presentation of Fantasy of Flight (above) to a real nuts-and-bolts operation. Working from a glory hole of a hangar-cum-workshop, surrounded by chunks of Flying Fortress, engines, propellors and wings, owner Tom Reilly and his team are the wizards of World War II aircraft restoration. Apparently irreparable bomber hulks are wheeled in and then resurrected to rise phoenix-like from the airstrip and go on to star in airshows around the country.

Every hour or so, a guided tour takes off around the museum and visitors are showered with information about the planes and their part in history. Practically everything can be touched – though woe betide any sticky fingers found smudging the fuselage of a fully restored Mustang. Several of the heftier restoration projects are lined up on the tarmac outside.

🕇 29B1
✉ 231 Hoagland Boulevard (NM 15.5), Kissimmee
☎ (407) 933 1942
🕐 Mon–Sat 9–6, Sun 9–5. Closed Chistmas and Thanksgiving
♿ Few
🍴 Cheap
↔ Congo River Golf (➤ 52), Jungleland (➤ 55)
❓ Aeroplane sight-seeing rides in an original 1934 Waco YMF-5 biplane painted to look like Snoopy's *Red Baron*: 40-minute, 25-minute and 15-minute rides

A Tour Around Mount Dora

Distance
60 miles round trip

Time
A 50-minute drive from Orlando. Allow half a day to look around Mount Dora

Start/end point
Orlando
✚ 46B2

Destination
Mount Dora
✚ 46B3

Lunch
Windsor Rose English Tea Room (£)
✉ 144 W 4th Avenue
☎ (352) 735 2551

A pretty lakeshore town set amid gentle countryside and citrus groves, Mount Dora is renowned for its Victorian architecture and antiques shops.

From Orlando, take the Orange Blossom Trail/US441 north (direction Ocala) to Mount Dora, and follow signs for downtown.

Northern settlers first arrived on the shores of Lake Dora in the 1870s, and built their town on a low rise overlooking the eastern end of lake. The oldest surviving building in town is the 1883 Lakeside Inn, 100 Alexander Street, a short step away from the Chamber of Commerce.

At the Chamber of Commerce, 341 Alexander Street (☎ (352) 383 2165), pick up a driving map indicating a three-mile route around the pick of Mount Dora's historic homes and buildings.

The attractively restored downtown district is fun to explore. It is only a couple of blocks, but many of the old buildings house art galleries, speciality gift stores, tempting gourmet food emporiums and the popular antiques shops. Also in downtown is Mount Dora's most impressive historic home, the splendid Queen Anne-style Donnelly House. Ornately decorated with ironwork, a cupola, copious gables, balustrades, balconies and yards of gingerbread trim, it now serves as probably the daintiest Masonic Hall in the land. Near by, the town's former fire station and jail houses the small Royellou

Donnelly House, a Queen Anne-style confection in the Mount Dora district

Museum, displaying local history exhibits. Down by the lake there is a nature trail in Palm Island Park; boats and bicycles are available for hire near the yacht club.

Return to Orlando on the US441 or SR46/I-4.

GREEN MEADOWS PETTING FARM ✪✪

A great treat for small children, who can find the theme park experience and crowds a bit overwhelming. Here they can scamper about safely, clamber on tractors, collect acorns for the pigs and encounter all manner of other farmyard animals on the two-hour tours which allow them to meet and touch calves, lambs, kids, turkeys and fluffy yellow ducklings. Every child can milk a cow (if he or she wants to), and enjoy waggon rides and pony rides.

Free-ranging guineafowl, peacocks and chickens peck and preen around the attractive tree-shaded compound, which provides good protection from the hot sun, and toddlers or babies can be towed around in miniature farm trailers. Picnickers are welcome, there is a sunny grassed area and a sandpit and slides offer further fun.

🕂 46B2
✉ 1368 S Poinciana Boulevard, Kissimmee
☎ (407) 846 0770
🕐 Daily 9:30–5:30 (last tour 4PM)
🍴 Snacks, sandwiches and cold drinks available (£)
♿ Few
✋ Moderate

JUNGLELAND ✪

An old-fashioned zoo with plans to expand and develop a more naturalistic setting for its impressive collection of big cats and jungle-dwelling monkeys, lemurs and colourful birds. In fairness, most of the big cats, including imposing Bengal tigers, lions, leopards and cougars, have been hand-raised, so are used to their confined quarters and respond eagerly to their favourite keepers. The beautifully marked Diana monkeys, ruffled vervets and entertaining lemurs, too, are quite at home, and on-site comedian, Radcliffe the orangutan, made his name on the big screen as Clint Eastwood's sidekick, Clyde, in *Every Which Way But Loose*. There are giant porcupines and mongeese, capybaras (the world's largest rodent), chatty macaws, mynah birds, cockatoos and kookaburras. Buy a bag of seeds and grains to feed down the plastic shutes.

🕂 29B1
✉ 4580 W US192 (NM 14), Kissimmee
☎ (407) 396 1012
🕐 Daily 9–6
♿ Good
✋ Moderate
↔ Congo River Golf (► 52), Flying Tigers Warbird Restoration Museum (► 53)

Above: *Green Meadows Petting Farm, a gentle alternative to alligators*

55

Food & Drink

Orlando knows a bit about mass catering. From sunrise to sunset and long into the night, the city's 3,000-plus restaurants, cafeterias, family diners and take-away operations aim to satisfy the hunger of a

Breakfast

For most visitors planning a long, busy day out and about sightseeing, the day begins with a traditional American breakfast, selected from a menu as long as your arm. Stockpile energy in the form of cereals, hot waffles or pancakes, served with bacon and maple syrup, eggs and hash browns, sweet fruit or bran muffins, toast or plain 'English muffins'. In general, hotel buffet breakfasts are reasonably priced, and several motels and suite hotels include a basic breakfast of cereal, muffins and pastries with coffee and fruit juice in the room price.

A typical American breakfast

Lunch

Lunch on the sightseeing trail often means alarming queues in the theme parks. The busiest time is between 12–2, and if you can manage to eat earlier or later it does make things easier. Guests who prefer a sit-down meal in a service restaurant at lunchtime should make reservations at the Guest Relations window when they arrive at the park. Otherwise there is usually a wide choice of eateries, from self-service cafeterias to hot dog stands, barbecue take-aways, sandwiches, burgers and ice creams, which can be eaten at outdoor seating areas.

Florida Specialities
Florida's two main food groups are commonly known as 'surf 'n' turf' – that's seafood and beef. There are dozens of seafood restaurants in Orlando serving fresh fish, crab, lobster, shrimp and other delicacies. Steak houses and barbecue restaurants also do a roaring trade, and there is plenty of Southern-style Cajun or Creole influence in dishes, such as tasty blackened chicken or fish coated in spices and cooked over the grill.

Dinner

The evening meal is a very flexible affair in Orlando. Some restaurants start serving at 4PM to cater for those who have missed out on lunch or determined budget eaters who make the best of 'early bird specials', discounted meals offered before the restaurants really begin to fill up at around 6:30–7.

The main non-Walt Disney World resort areas –

Above: *traditional ribs*

International Drive and Kissimmee – are well provided with inexpensive family restaurants and fast food chains, as well as medium-price range steak houses, American, Chinese, Italian and Mexican eateries. For something more up-market, look to the top hotels, such as the Peabody Orlando, for a chance to dress up and enjoy a gourmet meal in notably elegant surroundings.

Medium-price bracket and expensive hotels generally provide a choice of dining options, and this is certainly true of the Walt Disney World resort complexes. Restaurants serving up a selection of walking, talking oversized Disney characters along with their menu are a favourite with children, but do remember to book ahead to avoid disappointment (see panel, ► 97).

Delicious, freshly squeezed fruit juice – essential on a hot day

Drinking

Sightseeing is thirsty work in Orlando, and several rounds of soft drinks for the whole family at theme park or hotel prices can prove an expensive business. If you are on a budget, it is a good idea to stock up on bottled water, fruit juices or multi-packs of canned soft drinks at a supermarket. To buy or consume alcohol legally in the state of Florida, customers must be 21 or over.

A Tour Around Merritt Island National Wildlife Refuge

Distance
100 miles round trip; 120 miles as part of a day trip including Kennedy Space Center

Time
A 1¼ hour drive from Orlando; allow 40 minutes for the Black Point Wildlife Drive

Start/end point
Orlando
✚ 46B2

Destination
Merritt Island National Wildlife Refuge
✚ 47D2

Lunch
Take a picnic or eat at the Kennedy Space Center – restaurants, cafés, snack concessions (£–££)

In clear sight of the Kennedy Space Center's looming Vehicle Assembly Building (VAB), Merritt Island National Wildlife Refuge occupies 220 square miles of marshland wilderness harbouring some 300 species of birds and dozens of other types of wildlife.

Take the Bee Line Expressway/SR528 toll road east from Orlando to SR407 north. Follow signs for the Kennedy Space Center onto SR405. At US1, turn left (north) and drive through Titusville. At the junction with SR406, turn right, cross the Indian River, and continue to the entrance to the Black Point Wildlife Drive on the left.

The northern portion of Merritt Island is a rare natural habitat preserve spanning fresh- and salt-water lagoons, mangrove islands, oak hardwood hammocks and palmetto-covered sand dunes, providing food and breeding grounds for an enormous variety of native Floridian wildlife. Endangered species such as manatees, wood storks and bald eagles live here, and sea turtles come ashore to lay their eggs on the Canaveral National Seashore during summer.

Follow the seven-mile Black Point Wildlife Drive.

At Stop 1, a viewfinder points out bald eagles' nests; at Stop 5, hundreds of wading birds can be seen feeding on the mud flats at low tide; and the

This nature conservation area's habitats range from pocket-sized freshwater lagoons to vast saltwater estuaries

five-mile Cruickshank Trail, a circular walk from Stop 8, has an observation tower just a few minutes' walk from the parking area.

Return on SR406, then turn right on SR402 for the Visitor Center.

The Center provides more information about the Refuge, and a further choice of walking trails.

KENNEDY SPACE CENTER ●●●

The Kennedy Space Center offers a unique opportunity for the public to learn about the men and machines behind the US space programme, from its early beginnings in the 1950s right up to the present day. A visit comprises a number of elements, including narrated bus tours of the historic Cape Canaveral Air Station facility and the unmissable Kennedy Space Center tour, which includes a photo stop in clear sight of the landmark Launch Complex 39, and the giant Vehicle Assembly Building, where the shuttles are prepared. Visitors can stop off as long as they like at the new state-of-the-art Apollo/Saturn V Center with its excellent screen presentations covering the launch of Apollo 8, and a complete 363-foot-long Saturn V rocket on display.

Back at the main Visitor Center, IMAX theatres present a variety of space themed programmes, of which the earth-shaking launch close-up *The Dream is Alive* is still the best. Earthlings can wander around towering exhibits in the Rocket Garden, clamber aboard a full-size shuttle replica and discover a wealth of artefacts, from space suits and astronaut food to space capsules, in the Gallery of Space Flight.

See also ➤ 20.

🔲 47D2
✉ State Road 405, Merritt Island (Bee Line Expressway/SR528 toll road east from Orlando to SR407 north, and follow signs)
☎ (407) 452 2121 or 1-800 572 4636
🕐 Daily 9–dusk

Historic spacecraft in the Rocket Park

Did you know ?

French science fiction writer Jules Verne predicted Florida's space age future almost a century before NASA arrived on the scene. In his novel From Earth to the Moon, *published in 1863, Verne described 'Florida...shaken to its very depths' by the blast-off of a rocket called* Columbiad, *a name strangely similar to the* Columbia *orbitor launched in 1981.*

+ 46B2

Silver Spurs Rodeo
⊠ Silver Spurs Arena
☎ (407) 847 5118

Kissimmee Rodeo
⊠ 958 S Hoagland
  Boulevard
☎ (407) 933 0020
🕑 Fri 8PM–10PM

Old Town Kissimmee
⊠ 5770 W Irlo Bronson
  Memorial
  Highway/US192 (NM
  9.5), Kissimmee
☎ (407) 396 4888 or 1-800
  843 4202
🕑 10AM–11PM
🍴 Fast food, snacks, several
  restaurants (£–££)
♿ Few
🆓 Free
↔ Water Mania (➤ 66)

Above: Kissimmee, a
popular vacation base
south of Orlando, and a
few minutes from Walt
Disney World

KISSIMMEE ✪

First impressions of Kissimmee are not encouraging. The city limits stretch for miles along the US192 east–west cross route, either side of I-4, in a seamless run of billboards and small shopping centres, chain restaurants and low-rise hotels. The quiet downtown district, south of US192 at the junction with the Orange Blossom Trail (US17-92/US441), has been restored recently, but there is little here to interest tourists and it is rarely visited.

However, Kissimmee is a good location for budget travellers. This is the place to find reasonably priced accommodation close to Walt Disney World, and most hotels offer a free shuttle to the Disney parks. Inexpensive family restaurants are the order of the day along US192, and there are supermarkets for self-catering holidaymakers and plenty of family attractions close by. To help visitors find their way around US192, the city has erected a number of Navigational Markers (NM) along the highway. These are used in this guide to locate the various attractions.

A recreated turn-of-the-century Main Street, the **Old Town Kissimmee** open-air mall, provides an entertaining mixture of shops and half-a-dozen fairground rides, including the landmark Ferris wheel on the south side of Irlo Bronson Memorial Highway/US192. On Saturday evening a vintage and classic car parade is held here.

One of the top rodeo events on the professional Rodeo Cowboys Association southeastern circuit, the **Silver Spurs Rodeo**, takes place at Kissimmee biennially in February and July, and weekly demonstrations of calf-roping, bareback riding, steer wrestling and other cowboy and cowgirl skills take place at the **Kissimmee Rodeo** on Fridays.

See also Flying Tigers Warbird Restoration Museum (➤ 53), Jungleland (➤ 55), Water Mania (➤ 66).

LAKE TOHOPEKALIGA ⭐⭐

A short step from downtown Kissimmee, Lake Toho (as it is commonly known) offers an idyllic escape from the crowds. The 13-mile-long lake covers around 2,700 acres, with several islands in the middle where Seminole Indians once built forts. The bass fishing is excellent, and there is great birdwatching, with more than 120 species of birds living around the lake or visiting – like the winter population of white freshwater pelicans, who fly 2,000 miles south to escape the chilly northern temperatures.

The 30-foot *Eagle Ray* excursion boat takes passengers out on the lake from Big Toho Marina. Call **Aquatic Wonders Boat Rides** in advance and arrange for a half-day bass fishing trip with a knowledgeable guide, or a two-hour nature safari with a chance to see bald eagles, osprey, snail kites and more.

LAKE WALES ⭐

A quiet country town south of Orlando, Lake Wales is famous for the **Black Hills Passion Play**, an annual event since 1953, which comes here in February and runs to mid-April, including Easter Sunday. The story of Christ's last days on earth is played in an amphitheatre surrounded by orange groves, and draws considerable crowds.

The **Lake Wales Museum and Cultural Center**, housed in a former railroad depot on the main street, features local history displays and railroad memorabilia. The other local attraction is Spook Hill, more correctly known as North Wales Drive. Visitors who drive to the bottom of the hill and put their vehicle in neutral at the white line will find that they begin to roll uphill.

✚ 46B2

Aquatic Wonders Boat Rides
✉ 101 Lakeshore Boulevard
☎ (407) 931 6247

✚ 46B1

Black Hills Passion Play
✉ Amphitheatre (south of Lake Wales)
☎ Schedules and reservations: (941) 676 1495 or 1-800 622 8383

Lake Wales Museum and Cultural Center
✉ 325 S Scenic Highway (Alt 27), Lake Wales
☎ (941) 676 5443
🕐 Mon–Fri 9–5, Sat 10–4
♿ Few
💷 Cheap
↔ Bok Tower Gardens (➤ 47)

A beautiful Carolina wood duck, one of the many birds enjoying the waters of Lake Tohopekaliga

A Tour Around Ocala National Forest

Distance
95 miles round trip

Time
1¼ hour drive from Orlando.
Spend the full day in the
Forest, or also plan to visit
Silver Springs (➤ 22, 63)

Start/end point
Orlando
✚ 46B2

Destination
Ocala National Forest
✚ 46A4

Lunch
Take a picnic, or there are
snack concessions at
Recreation Areas within the
Forest (£)

Within the boundaries of this 366,000-acre woodland preserve, the world's largest sand pine forest rolls back from the banks of the St Johns River, sprinkled with nearly 1,000 lakes and criss-crossed by miles of walking trails. Hikers will find peace and quiet along the numerous woodland paths. Other popular pastimes include paddling one of the beautiful canoe trails and fishing on Lake Dorr.

Take the Orange Blossom Trail/US441 north from Orlando to the SR19 exit at Eustis. Follow SR19 north for 11 miles to the Visitor Center at Lake Dorr; the main Ocala National Forest Visitor Center is on SR40, 12 miles east of Ocala.

Stop off at the Visitor Center for a free map and browse among the leaflets giving information about hiking trails and short walks. The Center can also supply details of fishing, canoeing and boating locations scattered around the forest. Ocala National Forest is at the heart of Central Florida's Big Scrub country, one of the few places Florida black bears still inhabit. It is also an important native habitat preserve for deer, wild turkeys, eagles and owls. Wading birds are at home here too, easily spotted from boardwalk trails or around the lakes.

Head for Juniper Springs Recreation Area at the head of the seven-mile Juniper Creek canoe run.

This is a favourite spot, where canoe reservations can be made in advance (☎ (352) 625 2808). Other recreation areas, such as Alexander Spring and Lake Dorr, offer swimming, picnicking and boat hire.

Return to Orlando along the SR40, SR19 and US441.

REPTILE WORLD ★

Rather off the beaten track, east of St Cloud, this no-frills serpentarium's main mission is research, and the collection and distribution of snake venoms. There are cobra and viper venom-gathering programmes three times a day (at 11, 2 and 5), and meticulous notes cover each snake display. Discover the secrets of the rattlesnake's tail, learn how to distinguish the non-venomous scarlet king snake from the poisonous eastern coral snake (same black, red and yellow colouring in subtly different proportions), and contemplate the world's largest snake species, the reticulated python and the massive green anaconda, known to snack on crocodiles in its native South America.

🚹 46C2
✉ 5705 E Irlo Bronson Memorial Highway/US192, 4 miles east of St Cloud
☎ (407) 892 6905
🕐 Oct–Aug Tue–Sun 9–5:30. Closed Mon, Sep, Thanksgiving and Christmas
♿ Few
💰 Cheap

SILVER SPRINGS ★★★

A Central Florida sightseeing destination since the 1870s, Silver Springs has augmented its natural attractions with a host of rides, shows and other essential modern-day theme park ingredients.

Alongside the ever-popular boat trips and jeep rides, favourite shows include the Alligator and Crocodile Encounter, which showcases 13 species of crocodilians and a rare white alligator, and Reptiles of the World, starring one of the alligator's few natural enemies, a 110lb snapping turtle.

Swimming is permitted in the spring only during July, but for hot summer days the **Wild Waters** water park is conveniently located next door.

See also ► 22.

🚹 46A4
✉ SR40, 1 mile east of Ocala (72 miles northwest of Orlando)
☎ (352) 236 2121 or 1-800 234 7458
🕐 Daily 9–5:30 (extended summer and hols)
🍴 The Deli (£); Springside Pizzeria (£); Springside Restaurant (£–££); Swampy's Smokehouse Buffet (£–££); snack stops, ice creams and cold drinks stalls (£)
♿ Good
💰 Very expensive; no extra charge for concerts
↩ Ocala National Forest (► 62)

Wild Waters
✉ Adjacent to Silver Springs on SR40
☎ (352) 236 2043 or 1-800 234 7458
🕐 Mar–Oct daily 10–6, extended in summer
💰 Moderate

A Silver Springs resident: a passing racoon gives a friendly wave

A Tour Around Wekiwa Springs State Park & Wekiwa River

Distance
36-mile round trip to Wekiwa Springs: 54-mile round trip to Katie's Wekiwa Landing

Time
Orlando to Wekiwa Springs: 30 minutes; Orlando to Katie's Wekiwa Landing: 45 minutes

Start/end point
Orlando
✚ 46B2

Destination
Wekiwa Springs State Park
✚ 46B3
✉ 1800 Wekiwa Circle, Apopka
☎ (407) 884 2009
🕐 Daily 8–sunset 🎫 Cheap

Katie's Wekiwa Landing
✚ 46B3
✉ 190 Katie's Cove, Sanford
☎ (407) 628 1482
🕐 Daily 8–6

Lunch
Take a picnic; snacks and cold drinks in park; refreshments at Katie's Wekiwa Landing

The Wekiwa River is one of Central Florida's prettiest natural waterways. An unspoilt tributary of the St Johns, it flows on a lazy 15-mile journey north and east before emptying into the main river near Sanford. The river's headwaters rise in the Wekiwa Springs State Park.

Take the Orange Blossom Trail/US441 north from Orlando to Apopka, then head west on SR436. The entrance to the park is signposted on the left.

This is a lovely woodland park for walkers with plenty of shade and over 13 miles of hiking trails. The main loop trail visits a variety of different native habitat areas, from dry sand ridges to low, swampy areas close to the Rock Springs Run (be prepared for mosquitos in summer); there are several shorter loops, as well. Swimming is permitted in the refreshing main spring ('Wekiwa' means 'spring of water' in Creek Indian), and canoes are available for rental.

Another option for those interested in a guided boat trip is to approach the river downstream from the direction of Sanford.

From Orlando, take fast I–4 east to Exit 51. Then follow SR46 west for 5 miles to Wekiwa Park Drive, the side road leading to Katie's Wekiwa River Landing.

Guided canoe trips lasting anything from a couple of hours to a full day depart from the Landing, near the country store. There are no-strain electric boat tours, too, and individual canoes for rental. Call ahead for further information (see panel).

Return to Orlando along the SR46 and I–4.

SPLENDID CHINA ⭐⭐⭐

A ride-free zone where small is beautiful, Splendid China is a theme park with a difference. The speciality here is miniaturisation: 60 famous Chinese landmarks are rendered in unbelievable detail at a fraction of their original size.

Perhaps the most ambitious project is the Great Wall of China, rolling sinuously up hill and down dale for half-a-mile, dividing, as it was designed to do in the 3rd century BC, the civilized Middle Kingdom from the northern Barbarians (represented by a Mongolian Yurt exhibit). Another notably lavish undertaking is the Imperial Palace/Forbidden City complex.

Take a break from the sightseeing trail for the shows, and lunch Chinese-style at one of the on-site restaurants. The Chinatown marketplace, at the entrance to the park, has stalls and shops selling T-shirts and Chinese silk robes, embroidery, jewellery, wind chimes and fortune cookies.

See also ➤ 23.

🚩 29A1
✉ 3000 Spendid China Boulevard/NM 4.5, Kissimmee (3 miles west of I-4/Exit 25-B)
☎ (407) 396 8880 or 1-800 244 6226
🕐 Daily 9:30–7 (extended summer and hols)
🍽 The Great Wall Terrace (£–££); Wind and Rain Court (£–££); Pagoda Garden (£); Seven Flavours (£); Hong Kong Seafood Restaurant (£££)
♿ Very good
✋ Very expensive
🔄 A World of Orchids (➤ 46)

US ASTRONAUT HALL OF FAME ⭐⭐

Just down the causeway from the Kennedy Space Center, this is a popular stop with children, who enjoy the hands-on approach. There's lots of interactive fun here, along with space hardware exhibits from the Mercury and Gemini programmes and entertaining rides such as Shuttle to Tomorrow, a flight into the future aboard a full-scale mock-up of a 120-foot orbiter. Potential astronauts get to put themselves to the test with the G-Force Trainer, and another favourite attraction is the stomach-churning 3D–360° flight simulator ride – which is pretty good fun to watch as well.

🚩 47D2
✉ 6225 Vectorspace Boulevard/SR405, Titusville
☎ (407) 269 6100
🕐 Daily 9–5 (extended summer and hols)
🍽 Cosmic Cafe (£)
♿ Good ✋ Moderate
🔄 Kennedy Space Center (➤ 20, 59), Merritt Island Wildlife Refuge (➤ 58)

An astronauts' showcase

WATER MANIA ✪

Kissimmee's very own spash zone, this is the place to cool off in the height of summer or just enjoy a family day out. The 38-acre site features wave pools, lagoons, small children's watery fun areas and lazy inner tube rides on Cruisin' Creek. Thrill-seekers can shoot the body-surfing-style Wipe Out ride, the Screamer, the Double Berzerker, Twin Tornados, the blacked-out Abyss and curvaceous Anaconda. On a drier note, there are arcade games, mini-golf, beach volleyball and basketball, and picnic facilities.

WINTER PARK

A smart northern suburb of Orlando, Winter Park boasts a brace of fine art museums, an attractive shopping district and scenic boat trips on a chain of small lakes edged by millionaires' mansions. The town was originally laid out as a genteel winter resort for wealthy New Englanders in the 1880s. Its main street, Park Avenue, is lined with boutiques and art galleries, shops selling exclusive interior design knick-knacks and chic restaurants. On Saturdays, the local Farmers' Market, on New England Avenue, is a favourite stop for fruit and vegetable shopping and fresh-baked goods, or just browsing among the colourful stalls.

Morse Museum of American Art Pride of place goes to the gallery's world-famous collection of Tiffany glass, much of it salvaged from Laurelton Hall, Louis Comfort Tiffany's Long Island home, which burned down in 1957. Many of Tiffany's own favourite pieces are on display, such as the glorious Rose Window. There are earthy fruit and vegetable stained-glass still lifes, others depicting magnolia blooms and elegant wisteria lampshades. Further collections cover ceramics, furniture and metalwork, and Tiffany's contemporaries also get a look in, with glassware from René Lalique and Emile Galle, paintings by Maxfield Parrish, and contributions from Frank Lloyd Wright.

Rollins College and Cornell Fine Arts Museum

Florida's oldest college, established in 1885, Rollins' original campus buildings were constructed in fashionable Spanish-Mediterranean style on a pretty campus overlooking Lake Virginia. Near the entrance to the campus, the Walk of Fame features more than 400 stepping stones gathered from the birthplaces and homes of famous people, from Mary, Queen of Scots and Benjamin Franklin to Buffalo Bill. There is an attractive college chapel and theatre linked by a loggia, and the small but perfectly formed Cornell Fine Arts Museum housing notable collections of European Old Master paintings, 19th- and 20th-century American art, Indian artefacts and decorative arts (displayed on a rotating basis).

Opposite: *splashtacular fun at Water Mania*

Cornell Fine Arts Museum
- ✉ Rollins College, Holt Avenue, Winter Park
- ☎ (407) 646 2526
- 🕐 Tue–Fri 10–5, Sat–Sun 1–5. Closed Mon
- ♿ Good
- 💲 Free

Outstanding works of art can be found at the Cornell

Scenic Boat Tours

A chain of six little freshwater lakes around Winter Park is linked by narrow, leafy canals. The canals were once used to transport logs, but now facilitate the movement of small boats and allow scenic boat trips to putter from Lake Osceola down to Lake Virginia and up to Lake Maitland. The tours last about an hour and offer a prime view of Winter Park's most exclusive lake frontage - the grandest homes overlook Lake Maitland. Waterbirds are easy to spot and there is the occasional glimpse of an alligator.

Scenic Boat Tours
- ✉ 312 E Morse Boulevard, Winter Park
- ☎ (407) 644 4056
- 🕐 Daily 10–4, except Christmas
- ♿ Few
- 💲 Cheap

Walt Disney World

Walt Disney World is the apogee of the Disney phenomenon. It is a fairytale fiefdom, where litter and spoiltsports are banned and Cinderella Castle pops out of the storybook and into 3-D reality. Disney's appeal is universal. It makes nonsense of age and cultural barriers uniting people from all walks of life in the pursuit of good, clean family fun and escapist fantasy. Teams of 'imagineers' have resurrected everybody's favourite characters, then added the latest screen stars, state-of-the-art rides, shows and even gently educational exhibits spread over the three (soon to be four) main parks.

For some it is all a little too perfect, and Disney's reputation for ruthless efficiency leads to charges of blandness. However, the prime objective here is family entertainment and that, even the most grudging cynic would have to admit, Disney delivers in abundance.

'I have never called this art. It's show business, and I am a showman.'

WALTER ELIAS DISNEY,
(1901–66)

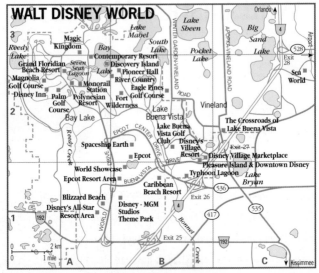

WALT DISNEY WORLD

Walt Disney World

The cooler winter months are the most comfortable time to visit Walt Disney World, and the crowds are definitely less pressing either side of the Christmas rush (January until mid-February, and mid-September until Christmas, with the exception of the busy Thanksgiving holidays). However, expect to queue whenever you go, and be well prepared with loose, comfy clothing, sturdy footwear and sunblock.

The Disney parks provide a wide range of guest facilities, from baby strollers and lockers to full-service banks and animal kennels. A limited number of wheelchairs are available, and there are special arrangements for sight- and hearing-impaired visitors. Information centres can also help with priority restaurant bookings, lost and found, camera rentals and free battery-charging.

DISNEY-MGM STUDIOS ⊕⊕
Disney-MGM Studios was Walt Disney World's riposte to the news that Universal Studios were opening a rival theme park-cum-studio facility at Orlando in 1990. Disney squeezed in just ahead, opening in 1989, and have almost doubled the size of the original park, though it remains rather shorter on rides than its chief rival. However, there is plenty of Disney flair on display and constantly updated exhibits showcase popular new productions, and give a chance to watch Disney's skilled animators at work.

❓ Details of daily parades, showtimes and nighttime fireworks and laser displays are printed in current park guides. Tickets are available on a one-day, one-park basis. Savings on the Four-Day Value Pass (one park each day) and Four-Day Park-Hopper Pass (any combination of parks each day), covering the three main parks, are minimal. For longer stays, the Five-Day World-Hopper Pass is good value, allowing unlimited entry to all main theme parks and water parks

---

✚ 29A1

✉ Walt Disney World, Lake Buena Vista (I-4/Exits 25-B and 26-B, 20 miles south of Orlando)

☎ (407) 939 7727

🕐 Check current schedules

Did you know ?

In spring 1998, Walt Disney World is scheduled to launch two cruise ships and a fourth full-scale theme park, Disney's Animal Kingdom. The fourth park will be Disney's largest ever, five times the size of the Magic Kingdom, and will combine thrill rides with exotic landscapes and over a thousand wild animals.

Each park offers a wide choice of dining options open for breakfast, lunch, dinner, and snacks throughout the day. Priority seating (bookings service at Guest Relations) is advised for table service restaurants (££–£££)

Free shuttle bus services from many Orlando/ Kissimmee hotels

Excellent

Very expensive

Backlot Tour After a visit to the splash tank and a chance to participate in a demonstration of special effects at sea, hop aboard a tram to cruise past the Star's Parking Lot, the world's largest working wardrobe department, the props and special effects departments. There are a couple of surprises in store at Catastrophe Canyon before arriving at the American Film Institute Showcase for a display of prize props and film memorabilia.

© Disney Enterprises, Inc.

Backstage Pass to *101 Dalmatians* A walking tour that explains many of the amazing special effects used in the 1996 block-buster. Meet mechanical animal stunt doubles and admire Cruella de Vil's *outré* props.

Great Movie Ride On Hollywood Boulevard, a full-scale re-creation of the famous Mann's Chinese Theater is the setting for this ambitious homage to movie classics. Audio-Animatronics® figures replace the great stars in famous screen scenes.

Take the fascinating Backstage Pass to 101 Dalmatians *walking tour*

Fascinating Facts

If you washed and dried one load of laundry every day for 33 years, you would clean as much as the Walt Disney World Laundry handles in a single day.

Around 450,000 miles of lawn are mown at Walt Disney World each year: the equivalent of 18 trips around the equator.

Enough Mouse Ear hats are sold every year to cover the head of every man, woman and child in Pittsburgh.

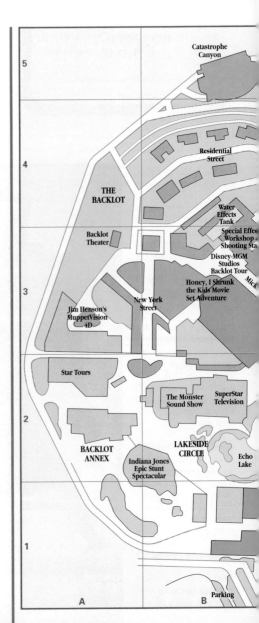

DISNEY-MGM STUDIOS THEME PARK

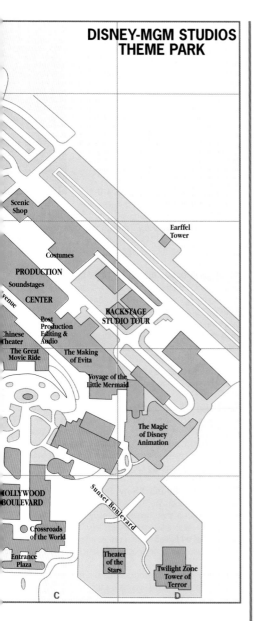

Scenic Shop

Earffel Tower

Costumes

PRODUCTION

Soundstages

venue

CENTER

Post Production Editing & Audio

BACKSTAGE STUDIO TOUR

Chinese Theater

The Great Movie Ride

The Making of Evita

Voyage of the Little Mermaid

The Magic of Disney Animation

HOLLYWOOD BOULEVARD

Sunset Boulevard

Crossroads of the World

Entrance Plaza

Theater of the Stars

Twilight Zone Tower of Terror

C

D

More Fascinating Facts

Guides at Adventureland's Jungle Cruise (➤ 82) fire off almost 631,000 rounds of blank ammunition every year. MGM–Disney Studios (➤ 70–5) is home to the all-new *Tarzan: The Epic Adventures* television series. Both Walt Disney World and Disneyland are built in counties called Orange.

Just like its famous namesake, Disney–MGM's Chinese Theater features the handprints of famous movie and television stars who have visited the studios. Look out for Alan Alda, Tom Cruise and Lauren Bacall among others.

73

Advance Information

✉ Walt Disney World Guest Information, PO Box 10,040, Lake Buena Vista, FL 32830-0040

☎ (407) 824 4321

❓ Copies of WDW *Guidebook for Disabled Guests* available

Transport across WDW

🚌 WDW buses (free to WDW Resort guests and multi-day pass holders) service the parks from the main Transportation and Ticket Center at Magic Kingdom; journeys take up to 90 mins

❓ The sprawling WDW site is difficult to negotiate, although the complex road system is well-signposted. There are considerable distances between the various parks and resort hotels, which make a car useful, though not essential.

Honey, I Shrunk the Kids An imaginative children's adventure play area featuring giant bugs, spider's web rope ladders, looming blades of grass and cooling water jets (✚ 72B3).

Indiana Jones® Epic Stunt Spectacular! Check schedules with the Action Planner section of the park's free giveaway map, and catch a performance of this explosive stunt show. 'Audience volunteers' get an opportunity to join in the fun (✚ 72B2).

Jim Henson's Muppet Vision 4-D Jim Henson's magnificent Muppets have made the quantum leap from 3-D to 4-D with a little bit of help from Disney's animatronic wizardry. A terrific combination of big screen 70mm, 3-D film action, monster special effects and anarchic humour. (✚ 72A3).

The Magic of Disney Animation A brief but illuminating insight into the world of animation which traces the long and painstaking road from a story idea to the finished product. Check out the original artworks in the animation gallery before Robin Williams and Walter Cronkite's jaunty introductory film. The tour leads off through the production studios, where artists crouch over their drawing boards, for a question and answer session with an in-house animator and a selection of scenes from animation film classics screened in the Disney Classics Theater (✚ 72B2).

The Making of Evita More behind-the-scenes intelligence, this time a documentary recording the making of Alan Parker's screen version of *Evita*. A slow start walking past silent post-production areas, but the film includes plenty of on-location footage and interviews with Parker, Madonna and Antonio Banderas (✚ 73C2).

The Monster Sound Show This amusing show challenges the audience to get creative and provide the sound track for a short mystery-comedy motion picture. The amateur audio artists select their 'tools' from a bizarre collection of odds and ends. Further interactive entertainment is on offer in the Soundworks area (✚ 72B2).

Star Tours A bone-shaking intergalatic thrill ride on a runaway space ship. Wild simulator action, dazzling special effects. The pre-flight warnings aimed at pregnant women,

heart condition sufferers and the faint-hearted should also deter anybody who has eaten recently (✚ 72A2).

Star Tours – hang on to your stomach!

SuperStar Television The perfect opportunity to gatecrash an episode of your favourite classic TV show through the minor miracle of bluescreen editing, a blend of live action and pretaped footage. Join the cast of *Cheers*, *I Love Lucy*, or Jay Leno's *Tonight Show* (✚ 72B2).

Theater of the Stars In a setting reminiscent of the Hollywood Bowl, the 1,500-seat Theater of the Stars hosts musical spectaculars guaranteed to appeal to audiences of all ages. Other stage shows starring favourite Disney characters appear at the Backlot Theater (✚ 73C1).

The Twilight Zone Tower of Terror® A quiet stroll down Sunset Boulevard is soon interrupted by the shrieks of terrified passengers plummeting down the lift shaft of the spooky Hollywood Tower Hotel. Guests encounter various mysterious manifesta-tions on the route to the top of the 199-foot building before the plunge (✚ 73D1).

Did you know ?

The liftshaft drop in the Tower of Terror, Walt Disney World's tallest attraction, is the equivalent of falling off the ears of the park's Earffel Tower. It takes just three seconds.

Voyage of the Little Mermaid Beloved of little girls the world over, Ariel (the Little Mermaid of the title) gets the full theme park treatment as her story is retold with a barrage of clever special effects, puppets, animatronics, film clips and live performers (✚ 73C2).

🕂 29A1
✉ Epcot Center Drive, Walt
Disney World

EPCOT ⊗⊗
Walt Disney's original plan to create a Utopian-style
research community living on the Epcot (Experimental
Prototype Community of Tomorrow) site never came to
fruition, but his ideas have been adapted to provide a semi-
educational showcase for new technology and sciences
and a window on the world around us.

Epcot, twice the size of Magic Kingdom, is divided into
two parts. In the shadow of a giant silver geosphere, the
Future World pavilions house the scientific stuff, with
displays focusing on transport, communications, health,
energy, agriculture and oceanology. This sounds rather
serious, but the Disney Imagineers have added plenty of
hands-on fun, rides and film shows. The second section of
the park is World Showcase, a 1.3-mile promenade
through 11 'villages' each representing the potted history,
culture and architecture of a different nation.

FUTURE WORLD
Horizons A sedate ride through 'past futures', or how the
visionaries of yesterday imagined life in the 21st century,
followed by similar speculations on desert agriculture,
video-phone links, undersea and space communities from
a late-20th century viewpoint. It has a dated feel, and it
appears that we have only a few years before fashion is
abandoned in favour of Star Trek-style jump suits
(🕂 78A2).

*Above: Honey, I Shrunk
the Audience is a 3-D
adventure full of surprises*

© Disney Enterprises, Inc.

Innoventions Tomorrow's technology today, as top companies preview their latest inventions in an interactive enviroment. Get to grips with Magnetic Resonance Imaging, which is set to replace the old-fashioned x-ray; step into cyberspace; experience virtual reality adventures and check out the latest computer technology (⊞ 78C2).

Journey Into Imagination A flight of fantasy in search of the sources of imagination in the company of an airship-flying Dreamfinder character and a friendly purple dragon called Figment. Plenty of creative opportunities for the Disney art department as passengers journey through a mad scientist's storeroom of ideas, fairytale and nightmare landscapes, but children find it dull and would much rather watch *Honey, I Shrunk the Audience*, an excellent 3-D film show in the film theatre (⊞ 79E3).

Recommended Epcot Restaurants

🍽 Coral Reef, The Living Seas

World Showcase

🍽 Chefs de France, France; L'Originale Alfredo di Roma, Italy; Nine Dragons, China; Teppanyaki Dining Rooms, Japan

❓ Make lunch or dinner reservations at Guest Relations on entering park

The Land There are two deservedly popular attractions here, starting with Living with the Land. This gentle boat ride journeys through various environments explaining how plants survive, then continues into a futuristic greenhouse world where some of the fresh produce served in Walt Disney World restaurants is grown. This is quite a sight as you glide past giant citrus trees laden with 9lb lemons (each capable of producing two pints of juice), and string gardens where cucumbers, eggplants and banks of lettuces grow vertically. Guests who would like a closer look at The Land's experimental greenhouses should sign up for **Behind The Seeds**, a behind-the-scenes guided walk tour (⊞ 79F2).

On the upper level of the pavilion, the Circle of Life Theater presents an excellent eco-conscious film show starring characters from *The Lion King*: Simba the Lion King turns Simba-the-Educator and talks Pumbaa and Timon out of polluting Africa with the Hakuna Matata Electric Disco Holiday Resort. Pretty hard-hitting stuff for Orlando.

Behind The Seeds

✉ Reservations at Green Thumb gift store, The Land pavilion

🕐 Tours (1 hour) depart every hour 10:30–4:40

💷 Small additional charge

The Living Seas This 6-million-gallon salt water marine exhibit is a favourite stop. The centrepiece is an amazing man-made coral reef inhabited by 5,000 colourful and curious tropical fish. Sharks, bottle-nose dolphins, sea turtles and manatees, Florida's endangered prehistoric sea cows, also feature (⊞ 79E2).

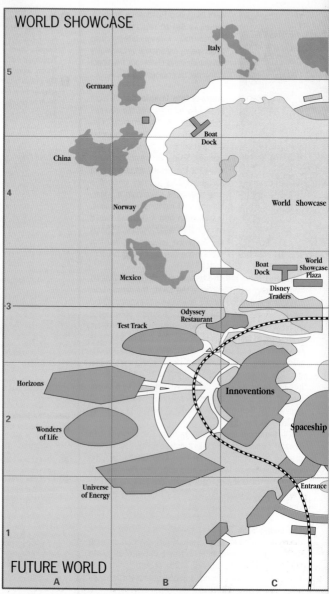

WORLD SHOWCASE

5

Italy

Germany

China

4

Norway

World Showcase

Boat
Dock

Mexico

Boat
Dock

World
Showcase
Plaza

Disney
Traders

3

Odyssey
Restaurant

Test Track

Horizons

Innoventions

2

Wonders
of Life

Spaceship

Universe
of Energy

Entrance

1

FUTURE WORLD

A   B   C

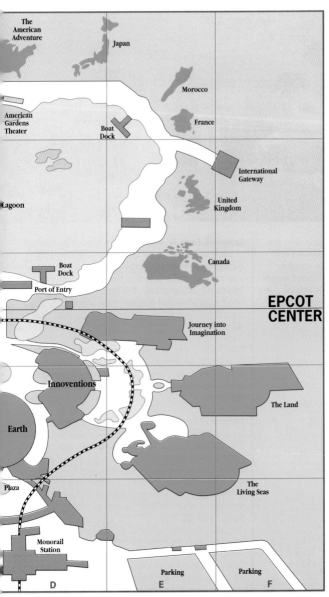

The American Adventure

Japan

Morocco

American Gardens Theater

Boat Dock

France

International Gateway

United Kingdom

Lagoon

Boat Dock

Port of Entry

Canada

EPCOT CENTER

Journey into Imagination

Innoventions

The Land

Earth

Plaza

The Living Seas

Monorail Station

Parking

Parking

D

E

F

Epcot's trademark – the silver Spaceship Earth geosphere – is a time machine in which you ride from the past to the stars

Spaceship Earth An entertaining ride through the history of communication inside the landmark 180-foot-high aluminium geosphere. Dioramas illustrate man's progress from cave paintings to a nifty neon journey down the Information Superhighway. Then passengers disembark into the AT&T Global Neighborhood and its diverting assortment of hands-on games with a futuristic flavour (⊞ 78C2).

Test Track The longest and fastest ride ever created by Walt Disney Imagineers features road test automobile action. Take to the track for a tyre-squealing, three-storey ascent and assorted high-speed manoeuvres in the dark (⊞ 78B3).

Universe of Energy Arguably the best ride in the park, this humorous romp back to the dinosaur era stars comedian Ellen DeGeneres in her own nightmare: an episode of the game show *Jeopardy* in which all the questions relate to energy. Cue Bill Nye, the Science Guy, who whisks Ellen (and the audience) off to a land of impressive animatronic dinosaurs for a lesson on fossil fuels. A CircleVision 360° film covers modern energy sources and *Jeopardy* is a piece of cake (⊞ 78B2).

Wonders of Life Humankind comes under the microscope in this pavilion, home to the entertaining Cranium Command show taking a look at the random workings of a 12-year-old boy's brain. The bumpy Body Wars thrill ride plunges through the human anatomy. Meanwhile, The

Making of Me handles human reproduction (parental discretion advised), and the AnaComical Players improvise skits on health issues (⊞ 78A2).

WORLD SHOWCASE
The American Adventure The centrepiece of the World Showcase villages presents a 30-minute dramatised history of America (⊞ 79D5).

Canada Feast the eyes on the CircleVision 360° *O Canada!* film and stock up on maple leaf motifs at a Rockies-style exhibit (⊞ 79E3).

China More CircleVision 360° scenic highlights, museum-quality displays of historic artefacts from Imperial China and elaborate architecture (⊞ 78A4).

© Disney Enterprises, Inc.

France Recreated Belle Epoque Paris in the shadow of a miniature Eiffel Tower. Café dining, wine-tasting, waterfront artists and a French perfumerie (⊞ 79E5).

Germany Storybook architecture with geranium-filled window boxes, plus traditional 'oompah' music piped out over the popular *biergarten* (⊞ 78A5).

Japan Wind chimes, temple drums and a pagoda, set beside manicured gardens and *koi* fish ponds, give an authentic twist to this shopping and dining complex (⊞ 79D5).

Mexico A huge model of a pre-Columbian pyramid and a boat ride down the River of Time attract plenty of visitors to the colourful Mexican village (⊞ 78B3).

Morocco An attractive Moorish souk set in narrow alleys and mosaic courtyards. Belly-dancing displays in the restaurant (⊞ 79E5).

Norway Malevolent trolls summon up a North Sea storm to rock the good ship *Maelstrom*, a Viking longboat thrill ride in this popular Scandinavian village (⊞ 78B4).

United Kingdom – or, rather, Merrie England: a jolly knees-ups with Cockney pearly kings and queens in the Rose & Crown Pub, and street entertainers massacring Shakespeare (⊞ 79E4).

Shop the World
The World Showcase villages offer unusual shopping opportunities. In Morocco's souk, genuine North African leatherwear, carpets, brass items and fezes make interesting souvenirs. Canada offers Indian and Eskimo arts and crafts; there are fine wines and porcelain on sale in the French village; Oriental goodies in China and Japan; and classic cashmere knitwear and Scottish tartans from the United Kingdom.

Epcot Entertainment
Throughout the day a range of shows, parades and cultural events takes place at locations around the park. Check current park guides for details of Mariachi concerts in Mexico, acrobats in Morocco, operetta in Italy and Caledonian bagpipe serenades in Canada. After dark, the 40-acre World Showcase Lagoon is the scene of the dramatic IllumiNations firework, laser light and sound spectacular, visible for miles around.

Transport to the Magic Kingdom

🚌 Shuttle buses pick up and drop off regularly at Transportation and Ticket Center

⛴ Ferry crosses Seven Seas Lagoon into Park; also monorail from Transportation and Ticket Center

MAGIC KINGDOM ✪✪✪

The Disney theme park that nobody wants to miss is, as a result, the most crowded, overwhelming and deserving of a second visit if you have time. Dominated by the fulsomely turreted and spired fairytale folly of Cinderella Castle, seven themed lands spread out over the 100-acre site, and there are 40-plus adventure rides, dozens of daily shows, and Disney characters at every turn.

Adventureland Lush tropical plants and eclectic colonial architecture set the scene for some of the best rides and adventures in the park. Explore the ingenious Swiss Family Treehouse, laid out amid the branches of a giant (plastic) banyan tree, and grab a pith helmet from the explorers' outfitters for a gentle rainforest Jungle Cruise complete with Audio-Animatronics® animals. The excellent Pirates of the Caribbean adventure is the most popular ride here, a rollicking boat journey into pirate territory with noisy special effects, one-eyed parrot-toting animatronics buccaneers, caves full of plundered loot and a marine attack on a Caribbean island. On a less bloodthirsty note, singing totem poles and flowers join feathered animatronic friends in terminally cute renditions of songs from South Seas musicals in the Enchanted Tiki Birds show (🔲 84A2).

Fantasyland Gathered at the foot of Cinderella Castle, rides and shows are based on storybook characters designed to appeal to smaller children. Classic fairground rides include the prancing, gilded horses of Cinderella's Golden Carrousel, the whirlygig cups and saucers of the Mad Tea Party and the two-man pachyderms of Dumbo the Flying Elephant. Children can cool off playing in the waterspouts at Ariel's Grotto; or float through the excruciatingly twee It's a Small World singing doll exhibit (🔲 85D4).

Frontierland A step back in time to the Old West with stores, a shooting gallery and a brace of good thrill rides. The runaway log flume action at Splash Mountain kicks up enough of a wave to cool off onlookers, while the Big Thunder Mountain Railroad takes passengers on a

whoopin' and hollerin' rollercoaster ride. Motorised rafts potter across to Tom Sawyer Island, a wooded domain which offers an undemanding Mystery Mine Shaft, lurching rope-and-barrel bridges, and short trails to the Fort Langhorn wooden stockade (✚ 84A4).

Liberty Square A genteel counterpoint to neighbouring Frontierland, Liberty Square has a more East Coast colonial feel and a patriotic spreading live oak, known as the Liberty Tree. Here, the worthy Hall of Presidents presentation tackles American history in a series of lectures delivered by Audio-Animatronics® US presidents. More lively by far are the undead in the Haunted Mansion. This schlock-horror ride through curtains of cobwebs, rattling bones and shrieking holograms is more rib-tickling than scary, but well worth braving the queues. In addition, there are boat trips on the Liberty Belle Riverboat or Mike Fink Keelboats; and good times galore at The Diamond Horseshoe Saloon Revue, which seems to have taken root here by mistake just short of Frontierland (✚ 84B4).

Shows and Parades

✉ Parade: Main Street, Magic Kingdom. Tribute shows: Castle Forecourt Stage, Fantasyland

🎟 Parades: daily 3PM

❓ SpectroMagic light show and Fantasy in the Sky fireworks held at nightfall

Dumbo the Flying Elephant – a traditional fairground ride for younger guests

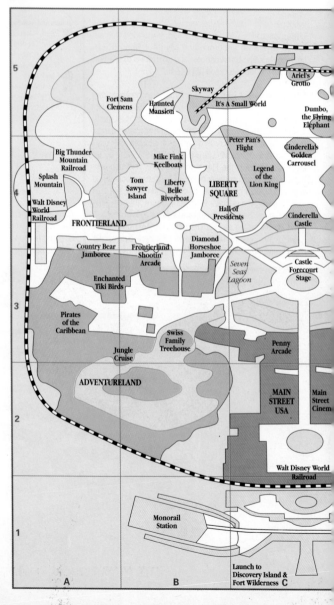

Map labels:

- Ariel's Grotto
- Skyway
- It's A Small World
- Dumbo, the Flying Elephant
- Fort Sam Clemens
- Haunted Mansion
- Peter Pan's Flight
- Cinderella's Golden Carrousel
- Big Thunder Mountain Railroad
- Mike Fink Keelboats
- Legend of the Lion King
- Splash Mountain
- Tom Sawyer Island
- Liberty Belle Riverboat
- LIBERTY SQUARE
- Walt Disney World Railroad
- Hall of Presidents
- Cinderella Castle
- FRONTIERLAND
- Diamond Horseshoe Jamboree
- Country Bear Jamboree
- Frontierland Shootin' Arcade
- Seven Seas Lagoon
- Castle Forecourt Stage
- Enchanted Tiki Birds
- Pirates of the Caribbean
- Swiss Family Treehouse
- Penny Arcade
- Jungle Cruise
- ADVENTURELAND
- MAIN STREET USA
- Main Street Cinema
- Walt Disney World Railroad
- Monorail Station
- Launch to Discovery Island & Fort Wilderness

5
4
3
2
1

A
B
C

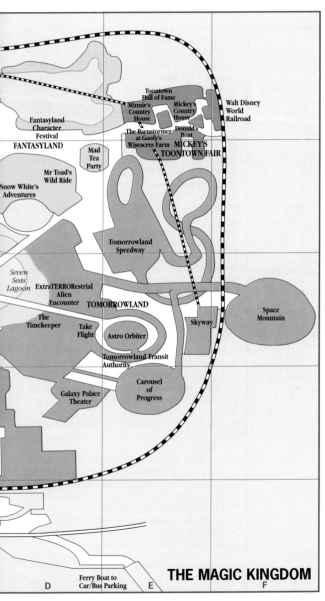

Toontown Hall of Fame

Minnie's Country House

Mickey's Country House

Walt Disney World Railroad

Fantasyland Character Festival

FANTASYLAND

The Barnstormer at Goofy's Wiseacres Farm

Donald's Boat

MICKEY'S TOONTOWN FAIR

Mad Tea Party

Mr Toad's Wild Ride

Snow White's Adventures

Tomorrowland Speedway

Seven Seas Lagoon

ExtraTERRORestrial Alien Encounter

TOMORROWLAND

Space Mountain

The Timekeeper

Take Flight

Astro Orbiter

Skyway

Tomorrowland Transit Authority

Galaxy Palace Theater

Carousel of Progress

Ferry Boat to Car/Bus Parking

THE MAGIC KINGDOM

D   E   F

85

Transport within the Magic Kingdom

🚉 Walt Disney World Railroad circles the perimeter of the park, starting at main entrance, with stops at Frontierland and Mickey's Toontown. Skyway cable car shuttles between Fantasyland and Tomorrowland; Tomorrowland Transit Authority loop ride operates within Tomorrowland

Cartoon Characters

✉ Disney Character Greeting Locations, highlighted on free map guides

☎ Schedules and reservations: (407) 939 3463

🍴 Character dining at The Crystal Palace (Main Street); Liberty Tree Tavern (dinner only, Liberty Square); character breakfasts in Fantasyland at Cinderella's Royal Table (reservations from the City Hall information centre)

Main Street, U.S.A. A prettified Victorian street scene, said to have been inspired by Walt Disney's childhood home in Marceline, Missouri, this broad avenue leads from the front gate up to Cinderella Castle at the hub of the park. Near the gates, City Hall is the main information centre and depot for the horse-drawn carriages and trams which trundle up Main Street to the castle. All along the route, shops sell a variety of Disney merchandise and gifts. There is an ice cream parlour, a bake shop and an old-fashioned Penny Arcade featuring authentic antique games. True Disney fans will want to stop off at the Main Street Cinema to catch a short spoof documentary film about Mickey Mouse in Hollywood and re-runs of vintage Disney cartoons (🚩 84C2).

Mickey's Toontown Home to Mickey and Minnie, this colourful corner of the park is a huge favourite with little children. Take a tour around Minnie's Country House, a symphony in lilac and pink hearts and flowers with a garden to match. Mickey's Country House, next door, displays wardrobes full of red pants, black jackets and big boots with Pluto's kennel in the garden. Children can cool off in the Donald's Boat play area, thoughtfully equipped with a bungee-soft floor and water jets; and there are pint-sized thrills on The Barnstormer at Goofy's Wiseacres Farm roller coaster (🚩 85E4).

Tomorrowland Dramatically updated and revamped, there is now lots to see and do here. Top of the list is Space Mountain, an old favourite and terrific roller coaster ride in the dark that many rate the top ride in the park. Tomorrowland Speedway is enduringly popular, too. A new thrill experience, The ExtraTERRORestrial Alien Encounter subjects the audience (trapped aboard an alien space transporter) to plenty that goes bump in the pitch dark (🚩 85D3).

On a rather gentler note, do not miss The Timekeeper, an amusing CircleVision 360° time travel romp hosted by a duo of smart-talking robots. Take Flight is a whimsy look at the history of flight. Take a real flight in the Astro Orbiter, a mini-rocket ship ride that resembles a chunk of 1950s space cartoon hardware, but does afford a good view of the area, as does the Tomorrowland Transit Authority, which detours into the bowels of Space Mountain to listen to the roller coaster passengers' screams. Debuted at the 1964 New York World's Fair, Walt Disney's Carousel of Progress has its fans, but in truth this stilted Audio-Animatronics® nostalgia-fest it is unlikely to appeal to anybody under 60.

Opposite: *Tomorrowland includes Space Mountain, Walt Disney World's star ride*

© Disney Enterprises, Inc.

Other Walt Disney World Resort Attractions

BLIZZARD BEACH ⊕⊕

Watersports are the speciality of Blizzard Beach, a northern ski-resort-gone-tropical water park, where the chair lifts sport sun umbrellas and the slalom course is a waterslide.

The 60-acre site boasts a dozen different adventure zones in the shadow of 'snow-covered' Mount Gushmore. Take a chair lift up to the 60mph Summit Plummet slide, or the slightly less dramatic Slusher Gusher. Other top attractions include the Teamboat Springs white-water raft ride, inner tubing down Runoff Rapids, and the Snow Stormers flumes.

On a less frenetic note, lazy Cross Country Creek circles the park and a sandy beach borders the wave pool below Mt Gushmore. Little children can play safely at Tike's Peak; and there is shopping for essentials and souvenirs in The Village, at the east end of the beach.

DOWNTOWN DISNEY ⊕⊕⊕

Downtown Disney is the new name for Disney's Lake Buena Vista shopping, dining and entertainment complexes which encompass the Disney Village Marketplace, Pleasure Island (see below), and the brand new Disney's West Side attractions.

Down on the lakeside, Disney Village Marketplace combines a selection of colourful boutiques and souvenir shopping outlets (► 106) with a host of good restaurants, including the landmark Rainforest Café (► 99), crowned with a smoking volcano. During the day there are pedal-boats for hire from the dock.

Opened in 1997, and still growing, Disney's West Side boasts the largest cinema complex in Florida, a state-of-the-art Virgin Records Megastore, and the Cirque du Soleil, a 1,650-seat theatre which opens in the fall of 1998 to stage glitzy, high-energy acrobatic and modern dance productions. Notable dining and entertainment venues include new Orlando outposts of the House of Blues and Gloria Estefan's Bongos Cuban Café.

PLEASURE ISLAND ⊕⊕⊕

A six-acre night-time entertainment complex, Pleasure Island's one-off admission ticket entitles guests to party the night away in any or all of its seven night clubs. There is also shopping, dining, movie theatres and dancing in the streets. Several of the shops are open during the day, when admission is free, but the real action (and paid

---

✚ 70A1
✉ W Buena Vista Drive, Walt Disney World
☎ (407) 824 4321
🕐 Daily 10–5 (extended summer and hols)
🍴 Lottawatta Lodge (£–££), Avalunch and The Warming Hut snack bars (£)
♿ Few
💷 Expensive (admission included with 5-Day World-Hopper Pass)
↔ Disney-MGM Studios (► 71–5)

✚ 70B2

admission) starts at 7PM and builds to a midnight New Year's Eve Street Party, complete with fireworks and a blizzard of confetti every night of the year. The action continues until 2AM.

The night clubs run the gamut from The Comedy Warehouse, with its nightly improvisational comedy shows, to the three-level Rock 'n' Roll Beach Club, which serves up live bands and DJs spinning hits from the 1960s up to the present day. Check out the laidback sounds and tapas bar in The Pleasure Island Jazz Company, or whoop it up in the Neon Armadillo, a top-rated country music venue and just the place to learn how to line dance. Lava lamps and mirror balls are all the rage at 1970s-style 8TRAX; for more contemporary sounds, hit Mannequins Dance Palace, which also features the gyrations of the Island Experience Dancers; and for something completely different, sample the interactive comedy and general weirdness on offer at the Adventurers Club.

- ➕ 70B2
- ✉ E Buena Vista Drive, Walt Disney World
- ☎ (407) 934 7781
- 🕐 Daily. Shops 10AM–1AM; clubs 7PM–2AM
- 🍴 Light dining in the clubs (££), also access to Disney Village Marketplace restaurants (▶ 97–8)
- ♿ Good
- 💰 Expensive (admission included with 5-Day World-Hopper Pass). Additional charge for movie theatres. Occasional additional charge for special shows in specific clubs
- 🔄 Downtown Disney (see above)
- ❓ Under 18s must be accompanied by a parent; for admission to Mannequins guests must be 21 or older. All guests need passport, driving licence or birth certificate to buy alcohol

© Disney Enterprises, Inc.

Pleasure Island has the nightlife scene covered

© Disney Enterprises, Inc.

🔲 70B2

✉ Fort Wilderness Resort and Campground, N Fort Wilderness Trail, Walt Disney World

☎ (407) 824 4321

🕐 Daily 10–5 (extended summer and hols)

🍴 Pop's Place (£), Waterin' Hole (£)

♿ Few

💰 Expensive (admission included with 5-Day World-Hopper Pass)

Above: Fort Wilderness is an excellent activities centre as well as the official WDW campground

🔲 70B1

✉ Epcot Center Drive, Walt Disney World

☎ (407) 824 4321

🕐 Daily 10–5 (extended summer and hols)

🍴 Leaning Palms (£), Typhoon Tilly's (£)

♿ Few

💰 Expensive (admission included with 5-Day World-Hopper Pass)

RIVER COUNTRY AND FORT WILDERNESS ✪✪

A suitably rustic-style water park located within Disney's 730-acre Fort Wilderness Resort and Campground. However, Tom Sawyer could probably not have dreamt up half the fun in store at River Country's Ol' Swimmin' Hole on the edge of Bay Lake. Cliffs of giant man-made boulders double as jumping and diving platforms, there are rope swings, water chutes, corkscrew flume rides and inner tube adventures. The smallest of the three Disney water parks, River Country gets very busy, but things do quieten down in the late afternoon and it is a great place to relax after a day's sightseeing.

Fort Wilderness offers an enormous range of outdoor activities, from watersports to horse-riding. Canoes and bicycles are available for rental; sign up for a game of volleyball or basketball; or just work on a tan down at the lakeside beach.

Another option is to take a picnic across to 11-acre Discovery Island. Exotic animals, walk-through aviaries and lush tropical gardens make a welcome escape from the crowds (➤ 109).

TYPHOON LAGOON ✪✪✪

A truly impressive water park complex with an artfully shipwrecked air, Typhoon Lagoon's showpiece is the 2.5-acre lagoon with surf-sized six-foot waves rolling onto sandy beaches every 90 seconds. Rocky Mount Mayday is landscaped with flumes and waterslides, and snorkellers can explore the 362,000-gallon salt-water coral reef environment, Shark Reef, inhabited by real tropical fish. For maximum thrills, check out Humunga Kowabunga, a 25mph, 214-foot waterslide. The rafting adventures are also highly recommended; and there is the separate Ketchakidee Creek water playground for little children.

Where To...

Orlando

Prices

Prices are approximate, based on a three-course meal for one without drinks and service:

£ = under $15
££ = $15 to $30
£££ = over $30

B-Line Diner (££)

Fun 1950s-style diner in the smart Peabody Orlando hotel (see Dux ➤ 93, and Peabody Orlando ➤ 101). Sandwiches, salads, pizzas and milkshakes are served; service is available 24 hours a day, and there is a take-out counter.

🖂 Peabody Orlando, 9801 International Drive ☎ (407) 352 4000 🕔 Breakfast, lunch and dinner 🚌 I-Ride, Lynx #42

Bergamo's (££)

This jolly Italian restaurant serves home-made pasta, fresh seafood dishes and steaks and other hearty dishes to the accompaniment of its famous singing waiters.

🖂 The Mercado, 8445 International Drive ☎ (407) 352 3805 🕔 Dinner only 🚌 I-Ride, Lynx #42

Bob Evans General Store & Restaurant (£)

Great American breakfasts on an heroic scale, then lunch and dinner to match in one of a chain of Bob Evans restaurants. Good value home-style cooking; cosy décor and apple pie atmosphere.

🖂 6014 Canadian Court, International Drive (north of Beeline Expressway) ☎ (407) 352 2161 🕔 All day 🚌 I-Ride, Lynx #42

Café Tu Tu Tango (£)

A jumbled artist's loft-themed dining room with genuine painters daubing away on site. You can order from a wide choice of multi-ethnic appetizer-size eats (tapas-style) and sample the sangria.

🖂 8625 International Drive

☎ (407) 248 2222 🕔 Lunch and dinner 🚌 I-Ride, Lynx #42

Charley's Steak House (££)

Voted one of the Top Ten Steak Houses in the US by The Knife & Fork Club of America. Prime aged beef cooked over a wood fire in a specially built pit. Good seafood, too.

🖂 Goodings Plaza, 8255 International Drive ☎ (407) 363 0228 🕔 Dinner only 🚌 I-Ride, Lynx #42

Charlie's Lobster House (££)

Fresh Maine lobster served eight different ways, a long menu of straight seafood and tasty variations such as the house speciality Maryland crab cakes. There is a good wine list and live jazz is performed.

🖂 The Mercado, 8445 International Drive ☎ (407) 352 6929 🕔 Dinner only 🚌 I-Ride, Lynx #42

Cheyenne Saloon (££)

Plentiful and scrumptious Western barbecue fare. Platters piled high with chicken and ribs, steaks or chilli, corn on the cob, biscuits 'n gravy. Frosted margaritas; very friendly staff.

🖂 Church Street Station (Brumby Building), 129 W Church Street ☎ (407) 422 2434 🕔 Dinner only except Fri, when the Cheyenne Backyard Barbeque brunch is served

Christini's Ristorante Italiano (£££)

Gourmet AAA Four-Diamond Italian restaurant. Classical cuisine with some light modern touches; one of the chef's star turns is *fettucini alla Christini.* Smart dress; charming service.

✉ **The Marketplace, 7600 Dr Phillips Boulevard/Sand Lake Road** ☎ **(407) 345 8770** 🕐 **Dinner only**

Copelands of New Orleans (££)

Spicy Cajun-Creole cuisine, grills and live jazz entertainment next door to the Mercado. The deep-fried onion appetizer is an experience.

✉ **8255 International Drive** ☎ **(407) 345 2220** 🕐 **Lunch and dinner** 🚌 **I-Ride, Lynx #42**

Coq au Vin (££–£££)

This one is something of a rarity: a Central Florida French restaurant which has a long-standing reputation for producing well-prepared classics in a relaxing atmosphere.

✉ **4800 S Orange Avenue** ☎ **(407) 851 6980** 🕐 **Tue–Sun lunch and dinner**

Damon's The Place for Ribs (££)

An old favourite for no-nonsense barbecued fare. Mouth-watering, juicy ribs are served up with the house special sauce and prime aged beef.

✉ **The Mercado/Suite 108, 8445 International Drive** ☎ **(407) 352 5984** 🕐 **Mon–Fri lunch only, Sat–Sun open 3PM–10PM** 🚌 **I-Ride, Lynx #42**

Dux (£££)

The Peabody Orlando's award-winning signature restaurant. Elegant décor, sophisticated New American cuisine and an excellent wine cellar are all part of the package. (Jackets for men.) The hotel also boasts a fine

Northern Italian restaurant, Capriccio, in a less formal setting.

✉ **Peabody Orlando, 9801 International Drive** ☎ **(407) 352 4000** 🕐 **Mon–Sat, dinner only** 🚌 **I-Ride, Lynx #42**

Hard Rock Café (££)

An Orlando outpost for the world's most famous rock café. The guitar-shaped complex at Universal Studios contains the usual impressive display of rock memorabilia including Elvis's Gibson guitar, the Beatles' 1960s suits and a surfboard autographed by Jan and Dean. On the menu, all-American burgers, hickory-smoked barbecue chicken, salads and the charmingly named house speciality, Pig Sandwich.

✉ **5800 Kirkman Road** ☎ **(407) 351 7625** 🕐 **Lunch and dinner**

Jungle Jim's at Church Street (£)

A veritable zoo of ceramic animal figurines greets visitors to this family-friendly downtown restaurant. The establishment has won awards for 'Orlando's Best Burgers' and 'Best Place for Kids'.

✉ **55 W Church Street** ☎ **(407) 872 3111** 🕐 **Lunch and dinner**

Lagniappe Café (£–££)

Authentic Cajun and Creole cooking is served here, including such filling fare as po' boy sandwiches, shellfish jambalaya, gumbo and delicious doughnut-like deep-fried beignets.

✉ **Bay Hill Mall, 7625 Turkey Lake Road** ☎ **(407) 354 0024** 🕐 **Daily 9AM–10PM**

Dux Delight

Ever since a couple of well-refreshed hunters jokingly popped their live decoy ducks in the fountain of the Peabody Memphis over a century ago, the Peabody people have had a thing for ducks. Twice daily (11AM and 5PM) The Peabody Orlando's marching mallards parade through the main lobby between their daily duties of circling the fountain and their $100,000 Royal Duck Palace. Take afternoon tea – and a camera! (➤ 101)

The Real Lili Marlene

German lyricist Hans Leip was on sentry duty during World War I when he began to write a song inspired by his girlfriend Lili, and his best friend's girl, Marleen. Finally set to music in 1938, *Lili Marlene* was already a hit in Germany when the Allies heard it on Nazi propaganda radio in North Africa in 1941, and adopted it as their own. Later US forces' sweetheart Marlene Dietrich made a celebrated version.

Lili Marlene's (££–£££)

Polished wood, gleaming brass and nostalgic World War I aviator memorabilia set the mood (see panel). Burgers and sandwiches at lunch; prime rib, seafood and other classics in the evening.

✉ Church Street Station (Exchange Building), 129 W Church Street ☎ (407) 422 2434 🕐 Lunch and dinner

Lombard's Landing (££–£££)

San Francisco-style seafood restaurant, all red brick and curly ironwork, overlooking the lagoon at the heart of Universal Studios. There is a big deck for outdoor dining, fresh seafood specials, pasta and burgers. Dinner reservations advisable in season.

✉ Universal Studios, 1000 Universal Studios Plaza ☎ (407) 224 6400 🕐 Lunch and dinner

McDonalds (£)

The world's largest McDonalds on the corner of International Drive. Whacky architecture incorporates built-in french fries. The usual burgers, plus pizzas and a video games room.

✉ 6875 Sand Lake Road ☎ (407) 351 2185 🕐 24-hours 🚌 I-Ride, Lynx #42

Ming Court (£££)

Stylish Chinese restaurant with views over neatly manicured Oriental gardens, mini waterfalls and koi ponds. Very good fresh seafood, and there are steaks and grills as well as skilfully prepared Chinese cuisine; *dim sum* trolley at lunchtime.

✉ 9188 International Drive ☎ (407) 351 9988 🕐 Lunch and dinner 🚌 I-Ride, Lynx #42

Old Munich Restaurant (££–£££)

No surprises here: authentic, fresh German dishes in a friendly atmosphere. Entertainment on Friday and Saturday evenings.

✉ 5731 S Orange Blossom Trail ☎ (407) 438 8997 🕐 Tue–Fri lunch and dinner, Sat–Sun dinner only

Olive Garden (£–££)

Popular chain of cheap and cheerful Italian restaurants at several locations around Orlando.

✉ 7653 International Drive ☎ (407) 351 1082 🕐 Lunch and dinner 🚌 I-Ride, Lynx #42

Popeye's Famous Chicken & Biscuits (£)

Popeye's New Orleans-style chicken comes with a mountain of fixins and side dishes including red beans and rice and a heap more.

✉ 6725 Sand Lake Road ☎ (407) 351 7041 🕐 Lunch and dinner (until late)

Race Rock (££)

Motor racing memorabilia and rock music in a heaven-sent dining opportunity for boy racers (see panel). First-class pizzas, pasta, burgers and fiery chicken wings.

✉ 8986 International Drive ☎ (407) 248 9876 🕐 Lunch and dinner 🚌 I-Ride, Lynx #42

Ran-Getsu (£££)

Authenic Japanese cuisine and an attractive location overlooking a Japanese garden and *koi* pond. Chefs prepare traditional *sushi*, *sukiyaki* and *tempura*. Entertainment at weekends.

✉ 8400 International Drive ☎ (407) 345 0044 🕐 Dinner only 🚌 I-Ride, Lynx #42

Around Orlando

Kissimmee

Giordano's of Kissimmee (£–££)

Family-friendly Chicago-style pizzeria also serving a selection of other favourite Italian dishes.

✉ 7866 W Irlo Bronson Memorial Highway/US192
☎ (407) 397 0044 🕐 Lunch and dinner

Hollywood Diner (£–££)

All-American 1950s-style diner with a monumental juke box. Nightly dinner buffet, cocktails and children's menu.

✉ Ramada Inn, 4559 W US192
☎ (407) 397 9333
🕐 Breakfast, lunch and dinner

JT's Prime Time

The all-you-can-eat Prime Rib Special is the mainstay of the menu at this budget family restaurant west of I-4. Also steaks and chicken, children's menu and games room.

✉ 8553 W Irlo Bronson Memorial Highway/US192
☎ (407) 239 6555 🕐 Lunch and dinner

Key W Kool's Oak Grill (££)

Nautical décor with a nod towards the Florida Keys and a steak and seafood grill menu fresh from the oak wood pit barbecue.

✉ 7725 W US192 (west of I-4)
☎ (407) 396 1166 🕐 Dinner only

Pacino's (££)

Family-owned modern trattoria serving homemade bread and operettas as well as good pasta dishes, seafood, and other Italian favourites.

✉ 5795 W US192 ☎ (407) 396 8022 🕐 Dinner only

Peking Gardens Restaurant (£–££)

Cantonese, Szechuan and Manadarin cuisine are all served up here. You can order from the full menu, or sample individual dishes from the buffet spread.

✉ 4160 W Vine Street/US192
☎ (407) 847 2266 🕐 Lunch and dinner

Ponderosa Steakhouse (£)

All-you-can-eat family restaurant chain featuring a groaning buffet table. Pay for an entrée then load up with soup, salad, pasta, chilli, shrimp, desserts, and much more.

✉ 7598 W Irlo Bronson Memorial Highway/US192
☎ (407) 396 7721 ✉ 5771 W Irlo Bronson Memorial Highway/US192 ☎ (407) 397 2477 🕐 Breakfast, lunch and dinner

Punjab Indian Restaurant (£–££)

Spicing up the dining options on US192, the Punjab serves tasty mild, medium and hot curries, as well as all the usual tempting Indian side dishes.

✉ 3404 W Vine Street/US192
☎ (407) 931 2449 🕐 Tue–Sat lunch and dinner, Sun–Mon dinner only

Red Lobster (££)

Popular seafood restaurant chain offering a wide choice of fresh fish dishes as well as seafood pasta, steak and chicken. Families are welcome; there is a special children's menu.

✉ 5690 W Irlo Bronson Memorial Highway/US192
☎ (407) 396 6997 ✉ 4010 W Vine Street/US192 ☎ (407) 846 3513 🕐 Lunch and dinner

Race Rock

Dine in the fast lane at this landmark racing themed restaurant with a distinctive checkered flag roof (► 94). Celebrity partners include Richard and Kyle Petty, Michael Andretti and Don Prudhomme. The foyer is a monument to high octane horsepower decked out with Formula One and Indy cars, dragsters, motorcycles, and speedboats. Video screens show racing footage, there are video games and, of course, a chance to stock up on Race Rock merchandise.

Picnics for the Park

Goodings, a well-stocked local supermarket chain, is the place to stock up for a picnic at one of the Central Florida state parks. There are branches at Goodings International Plaza (next to The Mercado), 8255 International Drive; and Crossroads of Lake Buena Vista, 12541 SR535 (opposite Hotel Plaza Boulevard). Concessions in the parks sell snacks and there are vending machines for cold drinks.

The Stagedoor (£–££)

Homesick Brits in search of pub grub and a warm welcome should make tracks for the former Rovers Return II. Steak and kidney pud and other old favourites on the menu; British beers. Children welcome.

✉ **9150 W US192, Clermont (west of Kissimmee)** ☎ **(941) 424 8056** 🕐 **Lunch and dinner**

Summerhouse (££)

Breakfast buffet followed by a day-long menu of tasty sandwiches, Mexican dishes, steaks and Cuisine Naturelle healthy options. Children 12 and under half-price.

✉ **Hyatt Orlando, 6375 W Irlo Bronson Memorial Highway/US192** ☎ **(407) 396 1234** 🕐 **Breakfast, lunch and dinner**

Tony Roma's 'Famous for Ribs' (££)

Popular chain with several locations in the Orlando area. Generous ribs, steaks, burgers, shrimp and chicken dishes. Children's menu.

✉ **3415 W Vine Street/US192** ☎ **(407) 870 9299** 🕐 **Lunch and dinner**

Lake Wales
Chalet Suzanne (£££)

Award-winning restaurant in a lovely country inn (▶ 103), Chalet Suzanne's cosy, antique-filled dining room overlooks a small lake. The excellent American-Continental menu is short, the wine list long, the service attentive.

✉ **3800 Chalet Suzanne Drive (off CR17A, 4.5 miles north of Lake Wales)** ☎ **(941) 676 6011 or 1-800 433 6011** 🕐 **Lunch and dinner. Closed Mon**

Mount Dora
The Beauclaire (££–£££)

Charming formal dining room in an historic lakeside inn. Gourmet dinner menu, but a more casual approach at lunchtime, when there are tables on the veranda and a choice of salads, light chicken and fish dishes. Popular Sunday brunch.

✉ **Lakeside Inn, 100 N Alexander Street** ☎ **(352) 383 4101** 🕐 **Lunch and dinner**

Windsor Rose English Tea Room (£)

Welcoming tea room with a gift and garden shop attached. Traditional Cornish pasties, Scotch eggs and Ploughman's (bread and cheese) lunches, as well as home-made scones and cakes.

✉ **144 W 4th Avenue** ☎ **(352) 735 2551** 🕐 **Morning coffee, lunch and tea**

Winter Park
East Indian Market (£)

An appealing market-cum-restaurant and gourmet take-out operation with a huge choice of pizzas, sandwiches to order, roasted vegetable and cous-cous salads and other treats. Indoor and outdoor seating.

✉ **610 W Morse Boulevard** ☎ **(407) 647 7520** 🕐 **Breakfast, lunch and dinner. Closed Sun dinner**

Park Plaza Gardens (£££)

An elegant New Orleans-style covered courtyard provides the setting for award-winning Florida cuisine. Creative dishes are served, employing the freshest local ingredients, there is a fine wine list and the service is exemplary.

Sunday brunch is a local institution.

✉ 319 Park Avenue South
☎ (407) 645 2475 🕐 Lunch and dinner

Pete's Bubble Room (££–£££)

Just north of Winter Park, this eccentric bric-à-brac-filled restaurant makes for an entertaining night out. Floor-to-ceiling 1930s–'50s memorabilia, huge portions and killer desserts.

✉ 1351 S Orlando Avenue, Maitland ☎ (407) 628 3331
🕐 Lunch and dinner

Walt Disney World and Lake Buena Vista

Arthur's 27 (£££)

International cuisine, elegant surroundings and panoramic views over the Walt Disney World night-time fireworks displays. A choice of *prix-fixe* menus as well as *à la carte* specialities. Reservations advised.

✉ Buena Vista Palace Resort & Spa, 1900 Buena Vista Drive
☎ (407) 827 3450 or 1-800 327 2990 🕐 Dinner only

Benihana of Tokyo Inc (£££)

Popular Japanese-American restaurant chain serving grilled steaks, seafood and chicken dishes prepared right before your eyes.

✉ 1751 Hotel Plaza Boulevard
☎ (407) 827 4865 🕐 Dinner only

Big River Grille and Brewing Works (££)

Visitors can watch beer being made and then sample the daily brew at Disney's very own on-site micro-brewery. There is outdoor seating and a casual dining menu.

✉ Disney's Board Walk, 2101 N Epcot Resorts Boulevard
☎ (407) 939 3463 🕐 Lunch and dinner

Bonfamille's Café (££)

Hearty American breakfasts give way to more spicy Creole cuisine at dinner time in this attractive courtyard restaurant. Spit-roasted chicken, seafood and prime rib are among the options.

✉ Disney's Port Orleans Resort, 2201 Orleans Drive
☎ (407) 939 3463
🕐 Breakfast and dinner

Bongos Cuban Café (££–£££)

Restaurant and nightclub created by Miami's disco queen, Gloria Estefan, and husband Emioil. Cuban-Latin American music and food.

✉ Downtown Disney
☎ (407) 828 0999
🕐 Breakfast, lunch and dinner

Brown Derby (££)

Faithful re-creation of Hollywood's famous Brown Derby restaurant. Comfortable 1930s-style décor.

✉ Disney-MGM Studios, W Buena Vista Drive ☎ (407) 939 3463 🕐 Lunch and dinner

Chef Mickey's (££)

Disney character dining guaranteed to delight the kids. All-you-can-eat breakfasts and a dinner buffet that kicks off at 5PM to accommodate a sensible bedtime after a busy day in the park (see panel).

✉ Disney's Contemporary Resort, 4600 N World Drive
☎ (407) 939 3463
🕐 Breakfast and dinner

Disney Character Dining

A sure-fire hit with children, there are plenty of opportunities to dine out with favourite cartoon characters. Minnie Mouse hosts breakfast at the 'Ohana in Disney's Polynesian Resort; Winnie the Pooh, Eeyore and Tigger tuck in at The Crystal Palace Buffet in Magic Kingdom; and Admiral Goofy and crew attend the Cape May Café breakfast buffet at the Disney Beach Club Resort. Check schedules and make reservations for these and other sightings (☎ (407) 939 3463).
Also ➤ 87.

Rainforest Café

A smoking, 65-foot-high mini-volcano in the middle of Downtown Disney? Unbelievable. But then so is the Rainforest Café, brainchild of Steven Schussler, entrepreneur and eco-warrior, who once moved all the furniture out of his house to improve the environment for his pet parrots. Immersed in the simulated rainforest, marvel at the live and animated wildlife, feel the creeping mist and be assured that all the ingredients are environmentally correct.

Chefs de France (£££)

Three top French chefs (Bocuse, Vergé and Lenôtre) provided the creative inspiration behind this up-market restaurant in Epcot's World Showcase. It is one of the most popular dining options in the park, so reservations are a must.

✉ **Epcot Center, Epcot Center Drive** ☎ **(407) 939 3463** 🕐 **Lunch and dinner**

Chevy's Mexican Restaurant (££)

Friendly service and good, fast Mexican food in a barn-like dining room. The sizzling mesquite-grilled *fajitas* are recommended.

✉ **Crossroads of Lake Buena Vista, 12547 SR535** ☎ **(407) 827 1052** 🕐 **Lunch and dinner**

Cozymel's-A-Coastal Mexican Grill (££)

Coastal Mexican seafood dishes are a speciality here, and they serve over 30 types of tequila. Lively atmosphere and outside dining.

✉ **12124 S Apopka-Vineland Road** ☎ **(407) 239 6644** 🕐 **Lunch and dinner**

Fireworks Factory (££–£££)

High ceilings, metal stairs and a realistic factory feel for this entertaining American barbecue restaurant. Smoked ribs, mesquite chicken, steaks and chops. Also fresh seafood and pasta dishes.

✉ **Downtown Disney (just outside Pleasure Island), 1630 E Buena Vista Drive** ☎ **(407) 934 8989** 🕐 **Dinner only**

Fulton's Crab House (£££)

Housed in a replica turn-of-the-century riverboat permanently moored to the shore of Lake Buena Vista, this seafood restaurant is popular so be prepared to queue for dinner. An enormous choice of expertly prepared fresh fish, a raw bar, and a notable sour cherry cobbler for dessert.

✉ **Downtown Disney (just outside Pleasure Island), 1670 E Buena Vista Drive** ☎ **(407) 934 2628** 🕐 **Dinner only**

Official All Star Café (£–££)

Glitzy new Disney eatery packed with all-star sporting memorabilia, wall-to-wall video monitors screening great sporting moments, pumping music and a menu featuring burgers, hot dogs, buffalo wings, steaks and ribs.

✉ **Disney's Wide World of Sports, 1701 W Buena Vista Drive** ☎ **(407) 939 5000** 🕐 **Lunch and dinner**

'Ohana (££–£££)

Polynesian-style family feasts served up in atmospheric South Seas surroundings with a barbecue firepit.

✉ **Disney's Polynesian Resort, 1600 Seven Seas Drive** ☎ **(407) 824 2000** 🕐 **Dinner only**

Orlando Ale House (£–££)

Casual nautical décor and big screen TVs for sporting events coverage. Steaks, ribs and seafood, plus 56 beers on tap.

✉ **12371 Winter Garden-Vineland Road** ☎ **(407) 239 1800** 🕐 **Lunch and dinner**

The Outback (££–£££)

Australian-themed restaurant with a three-storey waterfall and flourishing greenery, plus steaks, seafood and a storyteller recounting tales from the bush.

✉ **Buena Vista Palace Resort & Spa, 1900 Buena Vista Drive** ☎ (407) 827 3430 ⏰ **Dinner only**

Pebbles (££–£££)

Creative New American cuisine for the 'casual gourmet'. Delicious salads, seafood and poultry. Relaxed, friendly atmosphere. A local favourite with a second outpost in downtown's Church Street district.

✉ **12551 SR535** ☎ (407) 827 1111 ⏰ **Lunch and dinner** ✉ **17 W Church Street, Orlando** ☎ (407) 839 0892 ⏰ **Closed Sat lunch and Sun lunch**

Planet Hollywood (££)

Film and television memorabilia in all shapes and sizes from Keanu Reeves' bus in *Speed* to venerable collectables such as Gene Kelly's costume from *Singing in the Rain*. Brash, noisy, packed and planet-shaped; a convenient aperitif for a night out at Pleasure Island.

✉ **Downtown Disney (just outside Pleasure Island), 1506 E Buena Vista Drive** ☎ (407) 827 7827 ⏰ **Lunch and dinner**

Portobello Yacht Club (££–£££)

Generous Northern Italian cooking, featuring mountains of home-made pasta, pizzas cooked in a wood-burning brick oven and daily specials with the emphasis on fresh seafood. Bustling casual atmosphere and waterfront terrace dining overlooking Lake Buena Vista.

✉ **Downtown Disney (just outside Pleasure Island), 1650 E Buena Vista Drive** ☎ (407) 934 8888 ⏰ **Lunch and dinner**

Rainforest Café (££–£££)

Enormously popular jungle-themed restaurant swathed in deepest tropical décor. Trees and waterfalls, parrots and pina coladas. Broad menu of American favourites with a Caribbean twist (see panel).

✉ **Downtown Disney (Village Marketplace), 1800 E Buena Vista Drive** ☎ (407) 827 8500 ⏰ **Lunch and dinner**

Sassagoula Floatworks and Food Factory (£)

Mardi Gras parade props decorate this Disney budget dining option. American and Creole menu from burgers and pizza to fried chicken and sweet, deep-fried *beignets* (doughnuts).

✉ **Disney's Port Orleans Resort, 2201 Orleans Drive** ☎ (407) 939 3463 ⏰ **Breakfast, lunch and dinner**

Sum Chows (££–£££)

Fine contemporary Chinese restaurant which provides a less exotic children's menu, as well. Inquire about the house specialities – the giant butterfly shrimp in garlic sauce is recommended.

✉ **Disney's Dolphin Resort, 1500 Epcot Resorts Boulevard** ☎ (407) 939 3463 ⏰ **Dinner only**

Wolfgang Puck's Café (££–£££)

A Florida first for celebrity chef Wolfgang Puck, the man who popularized the designer pizza. His wood-fired pizzas feature the likes of smoked salmon, spicy chicken, Chinese duck and esoteric Italian cheeses.

✉ **Downtown Disney (West Side)** ☎ (407) 938 9653 ⏰ **Lunch and dinner**

Dining with Children

Not surprisingly, most Orlando restaurants welcome children. Family restaurants, burger chains and a wide choice of budget dining options abound around the International Drive resort area and Kissimmee. Many smarter restaurants are equally child-friendly and discounted children's menus are widely available; if you don't see one on display always ask.

Orlando

Prices

The following price bands are given on a per night minimum for a standard room regardless of single, double or multi-person occupancy:

£ = under $60
££ = $60 to 120
£££ = over $120

It is worth noting that many Orlando hotels make no additional charge for children aged 17 or under sharing with their parents, and provide double rooms which can sleep four people.

Arnold Palmer's Bay Hill Club & Lodge (££–£££)

A good option for golfers who would like to combine sightseeing with a challenging swing around Arnold Palmer's home course. Sixty-one rooms and suites; dining; pool and tennis.

✉ 9000 Bay Hill Boulevard (west of I-4/Exit 29) ☎ (407) 876 2429

Best Western Plaza International (££)

Well-equipped chain hotel midway down International Drive; 672 rooms and suites; pool; babysitting facilities.

✉ 8738 International Drive ☎ (407) 345 8195 or 1-800 654 7160 🚌 I-Ride, Lynx #42

Clarion Plaza Hotel (£££)

Elegant executive-type hotel close to the Convention Center; 810 rooms; pool; restaurants.

✉ 9700 International Drive ☎ (407) 352 9700 or 1-800 366 9700 🚌 I-Ride, Lynx #42

Country Hearth Inn (££)

Southern-style architecture makes a change from high-rise concrete: 150 modern, well-equipped rooms (children under 17 sharing parents' room stay free); heated pool; restaurant.

✉ 9861 International Drive ☎ (407) 352 0008 or 1-800 447 1890 🚌 I-Ride, Lynx #42

Days Inn International Drive (£–££)

Central chain hotel just north of Sand Lake Road with 240 budget rooms; pool; restaurant.

✉ 7200 International Drive ☎ (407) 351 1200 or 1-800 224 5057 🚌 I-Ride, Lynx #42

Embassy Suites Orlando South (£££)

Well-priced two-room suites sleeping up to six people in a central location. Pools; fitness centre; Family Fun Center; complimentary cooked breakfast.

✉ 8978 International Drive ☎ (407) 352 1400 or 1-800 433 7275 🚌 I-Ride, Lynx #42

Hampton Inn – International Drive Area (££)

Set back just east of International Drive and recently refurbished at a cost of $5 million; 170 rooms, all with fridge and microwave; pool; complimentary breakfast. Also a second location, near Universal Studios.

✉ 6101 Sand Lake Road ☎ (407) 763 7886 or 1-800 763 1100 ✉ 7110 S Kirkman Road (opposite Universal Studios) ☎ (407) 345 1112

Holiday Inn International Drive Resort (£–££)

Reliable budget- to mid-range chain with more than a dozen Orlando/Kissimmee locations: this one, near Wet 'n' Wild, has 644 rooms and suites; pools; restaurants; good children's facilities and baby-sitting services by arrangement.

✉ 6515 International Drive ☎ (407) 351 3500 or 1-800 206 2747 🚌 I-Ride, Lynx #42

Hostelling International – Orlando Downtown (£)

Not the most convenient location, but low rates and shared rooms in a pleasant Spanish-style building overlooking Lake Eola.

✉ 227 N Eola Drive ☎ (407) 843 8888

Hyatt Regency Orlando International Airport (££–£££)

Attractive airport hotel with direct access from the terminal; 466 spacious and functional rooms and suites; restaurants and bar; pool.

✉ **9300 Airport Boulevard** ☎ **(407) 825 1234 or 1-800 233 1234** 🚌 **Lynx #42**

Orlando Marriott (£££)

Landscaped garden setting for 1,064 rooms and suites. Choice of restaurants from fine dining to Pizza Hut; pools, lighted tennis courts and health club; good children's facilities, including a playground and baby-sitting services.

✉ **8001 International Drive (at Sand Lake Road)** ☎ **(407) 351 2420 or 1-800 421 8001** 🚌 **I-Ride, Lynx #42**

The Peabody Orlando (£££)

High-rise luxury (AAA Four-Diamond) opposite the Convention Center, with 891 attractive and spacious rooms and suites with a view; pool, tennis, health club; golf by arrangement. Restaurants including gourmet dining at Dux (▶ 93).

✉ **9801 International Drive** ☎ **(407) 352 4000 or 1-800 423 8257** 🚌 **I-Ride, Lynx #42**

Radisson Twin Towers Orlando (££)

Very reasonably-priced rooms and suites (760) near Universal. Excellent amenities include four restaurants; pool; shopping arcade; children's playground.

✉ **5780 Major Boulevard** ☎ **(407) 351 1000 or 1-800 327 2110**

Ramada Suites by Sea World (£££)

Well designed two-bed, two-bath suites (160) with fully equipped kitchens set in a resort complex with adjacent golf course. Fishing lake and paddleboats; volleyball; swimming pool; restaurants; children's playground; exercise centre.

✉ **6800 Villa DeCosta Drive** ☎ **(407) 239 0707 or 1-800 633 1405**

Silverleaf Suites (£)

Budget suite hotel near Universal Studios; 224 two-room efficiencies with kitchen and patio. Swimming pool, spa, fitness centre and tennis, plus picnic areas with barbecue grills.

✉ **5630 Monterey Drive** ☎ **(407) 295 0883 or 1-800 664 3633**

Summerfield Suites Hotel (£££)

Convenient for all the sights, as well as for the shopping and dining on International Drive: 146 one- to three-bed units which can sleep up to eight people. Swimming pool; bar; complimentary breakfast.

✉ **8480 International Drive** ☎ **(407) 352 2400 or 1-800 830 4964** ✉ **8751 Suiteside Drive, Lake Buena Vista** ☎ **(407) 238 0777** 🚌 **I-Ride, Lynx #42**

Travelodge Orlando Flags (£)

Budget option near Wet 'n Wild: 265 no-frills rooms; swimming pool; complimentary Continental breakfast; bar.

✉ **5858 International Drive (at Kirkman Road)** ☎ **(407) 351 4410 or 1-800 722 7462** 🚌 **I-Ride, Lynx #42**

Bookings

Reservations can be made by phone, fax or mail, and should be made as early as possible. A deposit (usually by credit card) equivalent to the nightly rate will ensure that your room is held until 6PM; if you are arriving later, inform the hotel. Credit card is the preferred payment method; travellers' cheques and cash are also acceptable, but payment may have to be made in advance. The final bill will include Florida's 6 per cent sales tax and local resort taxes.

Around Orlando

Spa Treatment

Footsore and weary after a day at Disney? The Buena Vista Palace's superb spa has the answer with its special Theme Park Foot Relief Massage. Spa guests (non-hotel residents welcome) can choose from a tempting array of more than 30 face and body treatments, ranging from aromatherapy to mineral baths. Book in for a single treatment or a half-day, full-day or weekend of luxurious pampering. Additional facilities include a Fitness Center, saunas, and beauty salon.

Kissimmee

Courtyard by Marriott Maingate (££)

The 198 rooms are newly renovated; pool and jacuzzi; fitness centre; dining; other restaurants and shopping within walking distance.

✉ 7675 W Irlo Bronson Memorial Highway/US192
☎ (407) 396 4000 or 1-800 568 3352

Econolodge Maingate Hawaiian Resort (£–££)

Aloha and welcome to this Hawaiian-themed budget option. Pool and restaurant, but no Disney shuttle service.

✉ 7514 W Irlo Bronson Memorial Highway/US192
☎ (407) 396 2000 or 1-800 365 6935

HoJo Maingate East (££)

Reasonably spacious rooms (567), including 83 'efficiencies' with fully equipped kitchens. Two pools and a playground; close to dining and shopping.

✉ 6051 W Irlo Bronson Memorial Highway/US192
☎ (407) 396 1748 or 1-800 288 4678

Homewood Suites Maingate at the Parkway (££–£££)

AAA Three-Diamond 156-suite hotel. Pool and spa; complimentary Continental breakfast; pets allowed.

✉ 3100 Parkway Boulevard
☎ (407) 396 4833 or 1-800 255 4543

Hostelling International – Orlando/Kissimmee Resort (£)

Central location with lake frontage and 166 beds in rooms and dormitories. Pool, laundry, Disney shuttles and bargain rates.

✉ 4840 W Irlo Bronson Memorial Highway/US192
☎ (407) 396 8282

Knights Inn Maingate (£)

Basic motel accommodation in 121 units a mile from Walt Disney World. Heated pool; free coffee; very low rates.

7475 W Irlo Bronson Memorial Highway/US192 ☎ (407) 396 4200 or 1-800 944 0062

Quality Inn Lake Cecile (£)

Budget option with central location close to shopping and dining: 222 rooms; lakeshore site, pool and watersports.

✉ 4944 W Irlo Bronson Memorial Highway/US192
☎ (407) 396 4455 or 1-800 864 4855

Ramada Inn Resort Maingate (££)

Full-service resort with 391 rooms on Walt Disney World's doorstep. Pool, tennis, restaurant and 'kids-eat-free' programme.

✉ 2950 Reedy Creek Boulevard ☎ (407) 396 4466 or 1-800 365 6935

Residence Inn by Marriott on Lake Cecile (££)

Very reasonable all-suite resort with 159 units. Fully equipped kitchens (including dishwasher); complimentary breakfast; pool and tennis; bar; baby-sitting.

✉ 4786 W Irlo Bronson Memorial Highway/US192
☎ (407) 396 2056 or 1-800 468 3027

Sheraton Lakeside Village (££–£££)

Family resort on a private lake with 651 rooms. Pool, tennis and paddleboats;

restaurant (free breakfast and dinner for children 10 or under with paying adult).

✉ **7769 W Irlo Bronson Memorial Highway/US192**
☎ **(407) 396 2222 or 1-800 848 0801**

Unicorn Inn (££)
English-style bed and breakfast in a restored historic home in the downtown district: 10 rooms with private bath; huge breakfast, home baking; helpful, friendly hosts; children welcome.

✉ **8 S Orlando Avenue**
☎ **(407) 846 1200 or 1-800 865 7212**

Lake Wales
Chalet Suzanne (£££)
Thirty large and pretty rooms spread around the grounds of a charming country inn. Peace and quiet, friendly and attentive service; very good restaurant (➤ 96).

✉ **3800 Chalet Suzanne Drive (off CR17A, 4.5 miles north of Lake Wales)** ☎ **(941) 676 6011 or 1-800 433 6011**

Winter Park
Langford Resort Hotel (££)
Well away from the hustle and the bustle, the family-owned Langford is a Winter Park institution: slightly aged, but homely and friendly with spacious rooms and a pool.

✉ **300 East New England Avenue, Winter Park** ☎ **(407) 644 3400**

Walt Disney World and Lake Buena Vista
Buena Vista Palace Resort & Spa (£££)
Luxurious and elegant hotel with 1,014 rooms/suites thoughtfully equipped with spa products (see panel).

Excellent recreational facilities; children's programmes; gourmet dining at Arthur's 27 (➤ 97).

✉ **1900 Buena Vista Drive**
☎ **(407) 827 2727 or 1-800 327 2906**

Disney's All-Star Sports and Music Resorts (££)
Two good value themed resorts; 3,840 rooms, each able to accommodate four adults; good facilities.

✉ **1701–1801 W Buena Vista Lake Drive** ☎ **All-Star Sports (407) 939 5000; All-Star Music (407) 939 6000; reservations (407) 934 7639**

Disney's Boardwalk Inn and Villas (£££)
Smart New England-style waterfront resort offering 378 rooms and 532 one-, two- and three-bedroom studios and villas sleeping 4–12 adults. Sporting facilities; children's activities; dining and shopping.

✉ **2101 N Epcot Resorts Boulevard** ☎ **(407) 939 5100; reservations (407) 934 7639**

Disney's Port Orleans Resort (£££)
Mid-range Disney hotel with an attractive New Orleans-style setting providing 1,008 rooms in three-storey buildings. Swimming, tennis and boating; restaurants.

✉ **2201 Orleans Drive**
☎ **(407) 934 5000; reservations (407) 934 7639**

Fort Wilderness Campground (£)
Woodland camp site offering hook-up facilities and cabins which can sleep six (£££).

✉ **4510 N Fort Wilderness Trail**
☎ **(407) 824 2900; reservations (407) 934 7639**

Budget Tips
Most hotels offer accommodation in several price ranges. If you are on a budget and the hotel rate offered is at the top end of your limit, always check to see if there is anything cheaper. If you are prepared to take a chance (not advisable in high season), many hotels are prepared to negotiate on the room price if they still have vacancies later in the day (after 6PM or so).

Shopping Districts & Malls

Mall Wonders
The Florida Mall is the biggest shopping experience in Orlando, anchored by outposts of the Saks Fifth Avenue, Sears, JC Penney, Gayfers and Dillards department stores. Popular brand-name fashion boutiques include Gap, The Limited, Benetton and Banana Republic, and there is a well-stocked Warner Bros Studio Store (➤ 106). If all that shopping works up a hunger, take your pick from 30 refreshment and dining options in the Food Court.

Orlando
Church Street Station Exchange
In the heart of downtown Orlando, Church Street Station's Victorian-style mall houses 40-plus boutiques, gift and novelty shops (➤ 30–1).
✉ Church Street Station (Exchange Building), 129 W Church Street ☎ (407) 422 2434

The Florida Mall
Central Florida's largest and most popular shopping destination: 200 speciality stores, anchored by five department stores (see panel).
✉ 8001 S Orange Blossom Trail/US441 ☎ (407) 851 6255 🚌 Lynx #42

The Mercado
A landmark tower sprouts above this Mediterranean-style marketplace. Some 60 speciality shops and restaurants set around an open-air courtyard with occasional live entertainment.
✉ 8445 International Drive ☎ (407) 345 9337 🚌 I-Ride, Lynx #42

Orlando Fashion Square Mall
Among the 165 boutiques and shops are branches of Sears, Burdines, JC Penney and Gayfers department stores.
✉ 3201 E Colonial Drive/SR50 ☎ (407) 896 1131

Pointe Orlando
A brand new up-market shopping and entertainment complex anchored by a branch of the FAO Schwartz department store. Megabook and music stores.
✉ 9101 International Drive ☎ (407) 352 3573 🚌 I-Ride, Lynx #42

Around Orlando
Kissimmee
Old Town Kissimmee
Around 70 souvenir stores, boutiques and gift shops, plus restaurants and amusement rides (➤ 60).
✉ 5770 W Irlo Bronson Memorial Highway/US192 ☎ (407) 396 4888

Winter Park
Park Avenue
An attractive downtown shopping district in the north Orlando suburb of Winter Park. Assorted boutiques, galleries, gifts and restaurants (➤ 66).
✉ Park Avenue (at New York Avenue) ☎ (407) 644 8281

Walt Disney World and Lake Buena Vista
Crossroads of Lake Buena Vista
Small shopping and dining complex at the entrance to Walt Disney World Village, with a useful branch of the Goodings supermarket chain.
✉ 12541 SR535 (opposite Hotel Plaza Boulevard) ☎ (407) 827 7300

Disney Village Marketplace
A fun place to shop and catch the breeze off Lake Buena Vista. Souvenirs, resortwear and World of Disney, the biggest Disney merchandise store in the world (➤ 106). Also restaurants, snack stops and boat hire from Cap'n Jack's Marina.
✉ Buena Vista Drive ☎ (407) 828 3058

Discount Outlets & Bargain Stores

Orlando

Belz Factory Outlet World
Two full-scale malls and four annexes containing 170 outlet stores selling cut-price clothing, footwear, sporting goods and accessories (see panel).

✉ **5401 W Oakridge Road**
☎ **(407) 352 9611** 🚍 **I-Ride, Lynx #8, 42**

International Designer Outlets
Just south of Belz (see above), designer fashion bargains from Esprit, DKNY, Off 5th-Saks Fifth Avenue, and others. Also Fila sportswear, china from Villeroy & Boch, jewellery and household appliances.

✉ **5211 International Drive**
☎ **(407) 352 3632** 🚍 **I-Ride, Lynx #8, 42**

Quality Outlet Center
A small outlet mall featuring American Tourister, Laura Ashley, Royal Doulton and Disney Gifts.

✉ **5527 International Drive**
☎ **(407) 423 5885** 🚍 **I-Ride, Lynx #8, 42**

Sports Dominator
Massive selection of sportswear, shoes and equipment from top names including Adidas, Head, Nike and Prince, with discounts of up to 50 per cent on selected items. Two locations on I-Drive.

✉ **6464 International Drive**
☎ **(407) 354 2100** ✉ **8550 International Drive** ☎ **(407) 345 0110** 🚍 **I-Ride, Lynx #42**

Around Orlando

Kissimmee

Kissimmee Manufacturers Outlet
Mini factory-outlet mall with 30-plus stores, including Nike, Cannon and American Tourister, offering 25–75 per cent discounts.

✉ **4673 West US192** ☎ **(407) 396 8900**

Sports Dominator
A Kissimmee outlet for this well stocked sports outfitters (see Orlando, above).

✉ **7550 W US192** ☎ **(407) 397 4700**

Osceola Flea & Farmers Market
Sprawling 900-booth flea market (Fri–Sun) specialising in souvenirs, dubious antiques and collectables. Also fresh local produce.

✉ **2801 E Irlo Bronson Memorial Highway/US192** ☎ **(407) 846 2811**

Sanford

Flea World
America's largest weekend market under one roof (Fri–Sun): 1,700 dealer booths and thousands of bargains on souvenirs, toys, household items and unbelievable tat.

✉ **US17-92 (4 miles southeast of I-4/Exit 50)** ☎ **(407) 321 1792**

Walt Disney World and Lake Buena Vista

Lake Buena Vista Factory Stores
Over 30 factory-direct outlet stores and a food court. Look out for 20–75 per cent off retail prices from the likes of Reebok, Swim Mart, Lee and Wrangler jeans from the VF-Factory Outlet, and the OshKosh B'Gosh Superstore.

✉ **15201 S Apopka-Vineland Road/SR535 (2 miles south of I-4/Exit 27)** ☎ **(407) 239 5429**

Bargain Belz
Resembling a giant shopping theme park at the top of International Drive, Belz is a magnet for thrifty shoppers. Bargain-hunters will find discounts of up to 75 per cent off retail prices on an enormous range of goods. Obviously, few items come that dramatically discounted, but there are considerable savings to be had on top brand products from Bally, Converse, Foot Locker, Guess?, Levi Strauss, OshKosh B'Gosh, Sunglass Hut, Van Heusen and many more.

Souvenirs

The Great Merchandise Heist

If theme park admission were not enough to lighten your wallet, dozens of alluring merchandise outlets make it easy to spend a second unscheduled fortune on souvenirs. One tip is to make a deal with children beforehand about what they can expect to take home (a T-shirt, a stuffed toy, a pair of Mickey Mouse ears etc) and stick to it. Visitors to Walt Disney World can also save valuable sightseeing time by avoiding the theme park stores and visiting the one-stop World of Disney superstore.

Orlando
Bargain World
Huge selection of cut-price Disney, MGM and Florida souvenir T-shirts, plus sportswear, swimwear and beach accessories.
✉ 6454 International Drive ☎ (407) 345 8772 ✉ 8520 International Drive ☎ (407) 352 0214 🚍 I-Ride, Lynx #42

Brumby Emporium
Western-themed souvenirs and apparel. Chilli motif boxers, tooled leather pistol belts and saucy garters for would-be gun-slingers and Diamond Lils.
✉ Church Street Station (Brumby Building), 129 W Church Street ☎ (407) 422 2434

Destination Orlando
Souvenir T-shirts with taste. Lots of neat, bright and original designs, good quality and all sizes.
✉ Church Street Station (Exchange Building), 129 W Church Street ☎ (407) 422 2434

Orlando Magic Fanattic
Souvenir merchandise from local NBA basketball heroes, Orlando Magic, and ice hockey team, the Orlando Solar Bears.
✉ 715 N Garland Avenue ☎ (407) 649 2222; also at the airport

Warner Bros Studio Store
Shelves piled high with cuddly and collectable souvenirs of Bugs Bunny and rest of the Loony Tunes crowd. Clothing, toys and accessories in all sorts of guises.
✉ Victorian Court/Unit 1013, The Florida Mall, 8001 S Orange Blossom Trail/US441 ☎ (407) 851 6255 🚍 Lynx #42

Around Orlando
Kissimmee
Bargain World
Two Kissimmee locations for Bargain World's discounted souvenirs and fashions (see Orlando above).
✉ 5781 W US192 (west of I-4) ☎ (407) 396 7778 ✉ 7586 W US192 (east of I-4) ☎ (407) 396 7199

Titusville/Merritt Island
Space Shop
Don't blow the entire souvenir budget on Disney – the Kennedy Space Center's souvenir shop is loaded with unusual mementoes. Astronaut food is a favourite, plus brilliant posters and T-shirts.
✉ Kennedy Space Center, SR405 ☎ (407) 452 2121

Walt Disney World and Lake Buena Vista
The Art of Disney
The place to find Disney posters, animation art, glossy art books and children's story books. Also at Disney-MGM Studios.
✉ Disney Village Marketplace, Buena Vista Drive ☎ (407) 828 3058

World of Disney
The world's largest Disney superstore. Just about the full range of Disney merchandise from adults and children's clothing to toys, jewellery and trinkets. Kids and kitsch-crazy adults have to be forcibly restrained from blowing the entire budget on Minnie Mouse slippers and Tigger baby-gros (see panel).
✉ Disney Village Marketplace, Buena Vista Drive ☎ (407) 828 3058

Miscellaneous

Orlando
a shop called MANGO
Florida Keys-style laid-back tropical resort gear, hand-painted shirts, Florida books and cards, plus the obligatory Jimmy Buffet tapes to transport you to Margaritaville.

✉ **Church Street Station (Exchange Building), 129 W Church Street, Orlando**
☎ **(407) 648 5222** ✉ **Old Town Kissimmee, 5770 W Irlo Bronson Memorial Highway/US192**
☎ **(407) 396 1336**

Great Western Boot Co
Authentic Western wear from Florida's largest Western store. Cowboy (and girl) shirts, jeans, hats, accessories and 10,000 pairs of boots.

✉ **Quality Outlet Center, 5597 International Drive** ☎ **(407) 345 8103** 🚌 **Lynx #8, 42**

World of Denim
Stock up on the top US brand name jeans and casual wear from Levi's, Guess?, DKNY, No Fear, and Timberland among many others.

✉ **8255 International Drive**
☎ **(407) 345 0263** 🚌 **I-Ride, Lynx #42** ✉ **5210 W Irlo Bronson Memorial Highway, Kissimmee** ☎ **(407) 390 4561**

Around Orlando
Cocoa Beach
Ron Jon Surf Shop
A local institution in this lively seaside town
(► 36–7). Nine acres of cool surfie beach gear, sand sculptures, board or in-line skate rental and café. Open 24 hours.

✉ **4151 N Atlantic Avenue/A1A (near junction with SR520)**
☎ **(407) 799 8888**

Kissimmee
The Last Great Hat Shop
Instant protection from the Florida sun. Genuine panamas, sequinned sun visors, cowboy hats and fun headgear in all shapes and sizes.

✉ **Old Town Kissimmee/Unit 305, 5770 W Irlo Bronson Memorial Highway/US192**
☎ **(407) 396 4871**

Shell World
Florida's oldest and largest retailer of seashells, coral and nautical knick-knacks: 50,000 shells from around the globe from less than a dollar to valuable collectables.

✉ **4727 W Irlo Bronson Memorial Highway/US192**
☎ **(407) 396 9000**

Walt Disney World and Lake Buena Vista
Character Christmas Shop
It is 25 December all year round at this Christmassy store laden with yule-themed gifts and decorations. Mickey, Minnie, Winnie the Pooh and other favourite Disney characters are all dressed up and ready for the festivities.

✉ **Disney Village Marketplace, Buena Vista Drive**
☎ **(407) 828 3058**

Wyland Galleries of Florida
Marine paintings, sculpture and prints from one of the world's leading environmental artists famous for his giant 'whaling wall' murals'.

✉ **Crossroads of Lake Buena Vista, 12541 SR535** ☎ **(407) 827 1110** ✉ **Disney's BoardWalk, 2101 N Epcot Resorts Boulevard**
☎ **(407) 560 8750**

Antiquing
Antiques-fanciers will find a few browsing spots around Orlando. East of Kissimmee, almost a dozen small antiques and collectables stores gather around New York Avenue in downtown St Cloud's quiet historic district. For more up-market pickings, try the smart antiques shops and galleries on Park Avenue in the prosperous Orlando suburb of Winter Park
(► 66). But the best antiquing opportunity around is downtown Mount Dora (► 54)

Alternative Attractions

Theme Park Survival Tips
The chief rule is: don't overdo it. Tired, overwrought children are bad company, so tailor your stay to their energy levels. Rent a stroller so that young children can always hitch a ride, and take plenty of short breaks. Walt Disney World Resort guests staying close by might consider making an early start, returning to the hotel for a rest and a swim, and revisiting the park in the cool of the evening (get a handstamp to allow readmittance). Be warned: many of the thrill rides are limited to passengers measuring 44 inches or more.

Orlando is all about children, but there are a few options other than the theme parks for younger visitors.

Orlando
Malibu Grand Prix Castle
Family entertainment complex with Go-Kart action, mini-golf, arcade games, baseball and softball batting cages.
✉ 5863 American Way (one block off International Drive) ☎ (407) 351 7093 🕐 Daily 11–10

Orlando Science Center
A state-of-the-art new science museum with dozens of interactive exhibits, film shows, a planetarium and 3-D laser shows (➤ 35).
✉ 777 E Princeton Street (I-4/Exit 43) ☎ (407) 514 2000 or 1-800 672 4386 🕐 Mon–Thu 9–5, Fri–Sat 9–9, Sun 12–5. Closed Thanksgiving and Christmas

Skull Kingdom
Step through a giant skull into this haunting new family attraction. Spooky, interactive walk-through exhibits culminating in the Ghoulish Face Painting Gallery.
✉ 5933 American Way (off International Drive) ☎ (407) 354 1564 🕐 Daily 12–2

Starbase Omega
Billed as 'the Ultimate Laser Tag Game', Starbase Omega is as good as its players, which can be pretty fast and furious. Part of the Mystery Fun House set-up (➤ 33), it also boasts Jurassic Park mini-golf.
✉ 5767 Major Boulevard (opposite Universal Studios)
☎ (407) 351 3356 🕐 Daily 10–9 (extended during season)

Trainland
A toy train museum with a large gauge indoor miniature train layout, and a gift and hobby shop.
✉ Gooding's Plaza, 8255 International Drive ☎ (407) 363 9002 🕐 Mon–Sat 10–10, Sun 10–6 🚌 I-Ride, Lynx #42

Around Orlando
Kissimmee
Fun 'N' Wheels
Family fun park with Go-Kart tracks, bumper cars and bumper boats, Ferris wheel, mini-golf, video arcade and bouncy Kiddie Port.
✉ Osceola Square Mall, 3711 W US192 ☎ (407) 870 2222
✉ 6739 Sand Lake Road (at International Drive), Orlando ☎ (407) 351 5651 🕐 Daily 10–midnight

Green Meadows Petting Farm
Farmyard fun for young children with pony rides and lots of animals to meet and pet (➤ 55).
✉ 1368 S Poinciana Boulevard ☎ (407) 846 0770 🕐 Daily 9:30–5:30

Horse World
Saddle up for a gentle nature trail or an excursion for more experienced riders through a 750-acre woodland preserve. Pony rides for little children.
✉ 3705 S Poinciana Boulevard ☎ (407) 847 4343 🕐 Daily from 9AM

The Ice Factory
Brand new ice-skating centre with two rinks and skating lessons. Skate rental and pro-shop, plus a children's

play area, snack bar and video arcade.

✉ **Partin Settlement Road**
☎ **(407) 933 4259** ⏰ **Daily 6AM–midnight**

Kissimmee Family Aquatic Center

A bargain alternative to the expensive water parks, this family pool is a great place to splash around, play on the scaled-down waterslide and lounge in the sun for a couple of dollars.

✉ **2204 Denn John Lane**
☎ **(407) 870 7665** ⏰ **Spring Break (late Mar) to end Sep; check schedules. Closed winter and Mon**

Pirate's Cove Adventure Golf

There are two 18-hole miniature golf courses with a buccaneering theme at each of these locations.

✉ **4330 W Vine Street/US192**
☎ **(407) 396 1556** ✉ **2845 Florida Plaza Boulevard**
☎ **(407) 396 7484** ⏰ **Daily 9AM–midnight**

Lake Monroe
Central Florida Zoological Park

Animal encounters in a Florida woodland setting among the live oaks and Spanish moss. Big cats, monkeys, birds and reptiles. Petting corner, picnic areas.

✉ **US17-92 (south of I-4/Exit 52 towards Sanford)** ☎ **(407) 323 4450** ⏰ **Daily 9–5, except Thanksgiving and Christmas**

Ocala
Don Garlits Museum of Drag Racing

A popular outing for boy racers – and their dads and mums: 46,000 square feet of automotive excellence from

muscle cars, hot rods and race cars to vintage Fords and a racing hall of fame.

✉ **13700 SW 16th Avenue (55 miles N of Orlando)** ☎ **(352) 245 8661** ⏰ **Daily 9–5**

Juniper Creek Canoe Run

Great for older children. The seven-mile canoe trail runs through the Ocala National Forest (➤ 62) and takes around four hours. Canoes can be rented in advance.

✉ **Juniper Springs Recreation Area, SR40 (22 miles east of Silver Springs), Ocala National Forest** ☎ **(352) 625 2802**
⏰ **Mon–Fri 9–noon, Sat–Sun 8–noon**

Titusville/Merritt Island
US Space Camp® Florida

Five-day live-in junior programme at the US Astronaut Hall of Fame (➤ 65). Open to children in grades four to seven. Budding astronauts study space science, launch model rockets and participate in simulated space missions.

✉ **Information from US Space Camp® Florida/US Astronaut Hall of Fame, 6225 Vectorspace Boulevard, Titusville, FL 32780**
☎ **(407) 269 6100 or 1-800 63-SPACE**

Walt Disney World and Lake Buena Vista
Disney's Discovery Island

A tropical bird and plant sanctuary on Bay Lake with animal species including Patagonian cavies (members of the guinea pig family) and giant Galapagos tortoises.

✉ **Access from Fort Wilderness Resort, 4510 N Fort Wilderness Trail** ☎ **(407) 824 4321** ⏰ **Daily 10–6**

Southern Belles at Cypress Gardens

Drifting around the floral displays at Cypress Gardens (➤ 52), like errant extras from the set of *Gone With the Wind*, the park's ringleted and crinolined trademark Southern Belles are many a little girl's dream. The Junior Belle Boutique, in the Southern Crossroads area, will transform junior misses (aged 3–12) into replica Southern Belles with make-up, hair-styling and a photograph to take home (additional charge).

Beyond the Theme Parks

Citrus Country

Thousands of acres of Central Florida are planted with citrus trees, but visitors rarely get a chance to stop and explore the groves. During winter (Nov–Apr), Ivey Groves Fresh Citrus, 2220 Boggy Creek Road, Kissimmee (☎ (407) 348 4757) offer daily orchard tours, and a chance to pick your own citrus fruits and sample free juices. At the Florida Citrus Tower (US 27 at Clermont, 23 miles west of Orlando), visitors are whisked up the 226ft observation tower for an unparalleled view of the groves below, which can also be visited on foot or by tram tour.

Orlando
Movie Rider Orlando

Movie simulator rides based on Hollywood all-action adventurer blockbusters, without the theme park queues. Giant screens, surround-a-sound and spine-cracking bucketing seats.

✉ 8815 International Drive
☎ (407) 345 0501 or 1-800 998 4418 🕓 Daily 10AM–midnight
🚍 I-Ride, Lynx #42

Terror on Church Street

Hair-raising high-tech special effects, in-your-face live actors and ghouls galore at this house of horrors near Church Street Station. Children under 10 must be accompanied by a parent or guardian.

✉ 135 S Orange Avenue
☎ (407) 649 1912 🕓 Sun–Thu 7PM–midnight, Fri–Sat 7PM–1AM

Around Orlando
Daytona
Daytona USA

Take a trip to the 'World Center of Racing' visitor centre at the famous Daytona Speedway. Racing memorabilia, excellent interactive displays and games, Pit Shop merchandise store and guided track tours.

✉ 1801 W International Speedway Boulevard/US92 (I-4/Exit 57, 50 miles E of Orlando)
☎ (904) 254 2700 🕓 Daily 9–5

Kissimmee
AJ Hackett Bungy

Thrill-seekers welcome. Plunge off the 75-foot-high tower and let the bottom fall out of your world.

✉ 5782 W Irlo Bronson Memorial Highway/US192
☎ (407) 397 7866 🕓 Daily noon–midnight

Aquatic Wonders Boat Rides

Two-hour and half-day boat trips on Lake Tohopekaliga (► 61). Fishing trips, birdwatching and sunset cruises.

✉ 101 E Lakeshore Boulevard
☎ (407) 931 6247 🕓 Daily from 9AM, by appointment

Boggy Creek Airboat Rides

Half-hour airboat trips into the Central Florida wetlands explore a 10-mile swathe of sawgrass and natural creeks on the look-out for wildlife. Night-time 'gator hunts by arrangement.

✉ East Lake Fish Camp, 3702 Big Bass Road (off Boggy Creek Road) ☎ (407) 344 9550
🕓 Daily 9AM–dusk

Fighter Pilots USA

A half-day flying adventure screaming around above Central Florida in a SF260 Marchetti fighter trainer alongside an F-16 pilot.

✉ Kissimmee Municipal Airport ☎ (407) 931 4333 or 1-800 568 6748 🕓 Daily 9–5

Kissimmee Rodeo

Kissimmee's cowboys and cowgirls compete in trials of old-fashioned skill and daring on Friday nights (► 60).

✉ 958 S Hoagland Boulevard
☎ (407) 933 0020 🕓 Fri 8–10PM

Sanford
Rivership Romance

Riverboat luncheon cruises and Friday and Saturday night dinner-dance cruises on Lake Monroe and the St Johns River. Popular with an older crowd.

✉ 433 N Palmetto Avenue
☎ (407) 321 5091 or 1-800 423 7401 🕓 Daily 8:30–5:30

Sports

Fishing
Orlando
Bass Challenger Guide Service, Inc
Full- and half-day fishing trips with all equipment and transportation provided.
✉ PO Box 679155 ☎ (407) 273 8045 or 1-800 241 5314
🕐 Daily, by arrangement

Around Orlando
Kissimmee
AAA Alligator & Big Bass Fishing
Custom bass boats and tackle for half-, full-day and night-time fishing trips.
✉ PO Box 422707 ☎ (407) 348 2202 or 1-800 882 8333
🕐 Daily, by arrangement

Golf
► 36–7.

Horse-riding
Orlando
Grand Cypress Equestrian Center
A wide variety of lessons and programmes, English and Western trail rides at this up-market hotel resort.
✉ Hyatt Regency Grand Cypress, One Grand Cypress Boulevard ☎ (407) 239 1938
🕐 Daily 8–5

Around Orlando
Kissimmee
Horse World Riding Stables
Woodland trails for experienced and novice riders (► 108).
✉ 3705 S Poinciana Boulevard ☎ (407) 847 4343 🕐 Daily from 9AM

Walt Disney World and Lake Buena Vista
Tri-Circle-D Ranch
Trail rides through the Fort Wilderness countryside (riders must be aged 9 or more). Also pony rides for little children.
✉ Disney's Fort Wilderness Resort, 4510 N Fort Wilderness Trail ☎ (407) 824 2832
🕐 Daily 10–5

Tennis
Orlando
Orlando Tennis Center
A good downtown budget option with 16 courts and good facilities.
✉ 649 W Livingstone Street ☎ (407) 246 2162 🕐 Mon–Fri 8–10, Sat 8–8, Sun 8–6

Around Orlando
Kissimmee
Orange Lake Country Club & Resort
Sixteen well-priced courts close to Disney; advance reservations are not always necessary.
✉ 8505 W Irlo Bronson Memorial Highway/US192 ☎ (407) 239 1050 🕐 Daily

Walt Disney World and Lake Buena Vista
Disney's Racquet Club
State-of-the-art clay courts, private and group lessons, tennis ball machines, or sign up at Players Without Partners.
✉ Disney's Contemporary Resort ☎ (407) 824 3578
🕐 Daily

Watersports
Orlando
Buena Vista Water Sports/Dave's Ski School
Water-ski lessons, Jet Ski and competition ski boat rentals, and tube rides for groups (see panel).
✉ 13245 Lake Bryan Drive ☎ (407) 239 6939 🕐 Daily

Watersports at Walt Disney World
Walt Disney World's numerous lakes and lagoons are ideal for messing about on the water. Most of the hotels have waterfrontage and marinas where guests can rent a variety of small sail boats, jet boats, watersprites and pedal boats. There is water-skiing from the Fort Wilderness marina, parasailing from the Contemporary Resort, and canoeing along scenic canals from the Fort Wilderness, Caribbean Beach, Dixie Landings and Port Orleans marinas.

111

Spectator Sports

Spring Training
While most of the country shivers in grim winter temperatures, sunny Central Florida is the ideal location for the nation's top baseball teams to get in shape for the forthcoming playing season. During Feburary and March, fans can catch friendly games and practice sessions from the Houston Astros at Kissimmee, and the Atlanta Braves at the new Disney sports complex. Elsewhere in Central Florida, the Detroit Tigers train at Lakeland and the Cleveland Indians at Winter Haven.

American Football
Orlando
Orlando Predators
Aspiring local Arena Football League competitors. Check listings in the local papers for details of forthcoming games.
✉ Orlando Arena, One Magic Place ☎ (407) 648 4444

Baseball
Orlando
Orlando Rays
The Florida Marlins are the state's only major league baseball team, but the 'Double A' Rays perform at Tinker Field Apr–Sep.
✉ 287 S Tampa Avenue
☎ (407) 245 2827

Kissimmee
Osceola County Stadium & Sports Complex
Spring training home of the Houston Astros (see panel) and host to numerous amateur and professional baseball events throughout the year.
✉ 1000 Bill Beck Boulevard (off E US192) ☎ (407) 933 5400

Basketball
Orlando
Orlando Magic
The downtown Orlando Arena is home to the local Eastern Division NBA contenders when they are in town.
✉ Orlando Arena, One Magic Place ☎ (407) 649 3200 or 1-800 338 0005 ❓ Tickets from Ticketmaster ☎ (407) 839 3900

Golf
PGA Events
Home to 30 PGA Tour pros and 11 LPGA pros, Orlando is Florida's golfing capital. Local courses host two annual PGA events: in March, the Bay Hill Invitational is played at Arnold Palmer's Bay Hill Club, 9000 Bay Hill Boulevard, Orlando (☎ (407) 876 2888); in October, Disney offer a million-dollar purse for the Walt Disney World/Oldsmobile Golf Classic contested on their Palm, Magnolia and Lake Buena Vista golf courses (☎ 1-800 582 1908).

Ice Hockey
Orlando
Orlando Solar Bears
Orlando's professional ice hockey team pucker up from September to April.
✉ Orlando Arena, One Magic Place ☎ (407) 428 6600
❓ Tickets from Ticketmaster ☎ (407) 839 3900

Motor Racing
Around Orlando
Daytona International Speedway
Home to the famous Daytona 500 and Speed Weeks race programme, plus various motorcyle events.
✉ 1801 W International Speedway Boulevard ☎ (904) 253 RACE; Bike Week and Biketober Festivals (904) 255 0415 or 1-800 854 1234

Sports Complex
Disney's Wide World of Sports
Transforming Orlando into a major sporting venue at a stroke, Disney's spectacular new 200-acre sports complex boasts world-class facilities for more than 30 sports, plus a speedway, and hosts a full calendar of national and international events.

Dinner Shows

Orlando
King Henry's Feast
In Orlando, Henry VIII celebrates his birthday every night with a four-course feast, juggling, sword-fighting, fire-eating, jolly minstrels and singing wenches.

✉ **8984 International Drive** ☎ **(407) 351 5151 or 1-800 883 8181** 🕐 **Nightly** 🚌 **I-Ride, Lynx #42**

Sleuths Mystery Dinner Theatre
Solve a whodunnit between courses at this small dinner attraction. Entertaining action with a comedy angle and plenty of red herrings, but dinner is a rather long-winded affair for those attending the second show.

✉ **7508 Republic Drive** ☎ **(407) 363 1985** 🕐 **Nightly**

Around Orlando
Kissimmee
American Gladiators Orlando Live
A 90-minute live action, muscle-bound show at the 1,600-seat Gladiator Arena.

✉ **5515 W Irlo Bronson Memorial Highway/US192 (NM 10)** ☎ **(407) 390 0000 or 1-800 BATTLE-4** 🕐 **Nightly**

Arabian Nights
A glittering equestrian spectacular, this is one of Orlando's main dinner attractions and combines over $5 million-worth of prime horseflesh with enough glitz to rival Las Vegas. Good all-round family entertainment and a real treat for horse-mad little girls.

✉ **6225 W Irlo Bronson Memorial Highway/US192 (NM 8)** ☎ **(407) 239 9223 or 1-800 553 6116** 🕐 **Nightly**

Capone's
An intimate 1930s speakeasy is the setting for this gangsters-and-molls comedy musical show. Good tunes, the small cast throws itself into the dance numbers with enthusiasm, and Bunny the Cigarette Girl steals the show.

✉ **4740 W Irlo Bronson Memorial Highway/US192 (NM 12.5)** ☎ **(407) 397 2378** 🕐 **Nightly**

Medieval Times
An evening of medieval spectator sports as dashing knights take part in action-packed horseback games of skill and daring, jousting and sword fights.

✉ **4510 W Irlo Bronson Memorial Highway/US192 (NM 14.5)** ☎ **(407) 239 0214 or 1-800 229 8300** 🕐 **Nightly**

Wild Bill's Wild West Dinner Extravaganza
Western-themed entertainment in a re-created 1870s cavalry mess hall. Knife-throwers, lariat-twirlers, bowmen, comedy turns and can-can saloon girls in a well-balanced family show.

✉ **5260 W Irlo Bronson Memorial Highway/US192 (NM 10.5)** ☎ **(407) 351 5151 or 1-800 883 8181** 🕐 **Nightly**

Walt Disney World and Lake Buena Vista
Hoop De Doo Musical Revue
Enormously popular Disney country-style hoe-down with sing-along tunes and a good all-you-can-eat barbecue banquet. Three shows nightly; advance reservations a must.

✉ **Disney's Fort Wilderness Resort, 4510 N Fort Wilderness Trail** ☎ **(407) 939 3463** 🕐 **Nightly**

The Bottom Line
Dinner shows are enormously popular, but they are not cheap. The average price for dinner (including unlimited wine, beer and non-alcoholic drinks) and a show is around $40 per adult. And, let's be honest, dinner theatres are not in the business of gourmet dining. Food is generally plentiful, but indifferent, tepid and occasionally inedible. The trick is to ignore promising menu descriptions and pick out the show most suited to your group of family or friends.

Live Music, Entertainment & Sports Bars

Stargazing

For a rather less conventional night out, the Orlando Science Center (► 35) invites stargazers to survey the universe through Florida's largest publicly accessible refractor telescope on Friday and Saturday evenings. On the same evenings, the Center also features laser light shows to rock music soundtracks and 3-D special effects in the world's largest Digistar II Planetarium, the CineDome (information, ☎ (407) 514 2114 or 1-800 672 4386).

Orlando

Blazing Pianos

Three fire-engine red pianos, the audience and a cast of singing wait staff belt their way through rock 'n' roll classics. Minimum age 21 Fri–Sat nights.

✉ The Mercado, 8445 International Drive ☎ (407) 363 5104 🕐 Nightly from 7PM 🚌 I-Ride, Lynx #42

Church Street Station

Downtown entertainment complex, where good times roll (► 30–1).

✉ 129 W Church Street ☎ (407) 422 2434 🕐 Daily to 2AM

Disney's BoardWalk

Live dance music from the 1940s to the 1990s at Atlantic Dance; duelling grand pianos at Jellyrolls; also the ESPN Club sports bar (minimum age 21 at Atlantic Dance and Jellyrolls).

✉ 2101 N Epcot Resorts Boulevard ☎ (407) 939 3463 🕐 Nightly

Friday's Front Row Sports Grill

Satellite sporting entertainment on tap, all-American menu and games room.

✉ 8126 International Drive ☎ (407) 363 1414 🕐 Daily until 2AM 🚌 I-Ride, Lynx #42

Howl at the Moon Saloon

Duelling pianos, sing-a-long rock 'n' roll favourites, loads of audience participation and party atmosphere. Minimum age 21.

✉ 55 W Church Street ☎ (407) 841 9118 🕐 Nightly until 2AM

Pointe Orlando

After dark entertainment at a choice of restaurants, clubs and a multi-screen cinema with an IMAX 3-D theatre.

✉ 9101 International Drive (at Republic Drive) ☎ (407) 352 3573 🕐 Daily 🚌 I-Ride, Lynx #42

Sak Theatre Comedy Lab

Best live comedy venue in Orlando. Award-winning improvisational shows at this downtown location.

✉ 45 E Church Street ☎ (407) 648 0001 🕐 Check schedules

Universal Studios Citywalk

Universal's new entertainment zone includes the Motown Café, the Down Beat Magazine Jazz Center, Bob Marley – A Tribute to Freedom, the NASCAR café and Pat O'Brien's Irish bar, as well as a brand new Hard Rock Café.

✉ Universal Studios, 1000 Universal Studios Plaza ☎ (407) 363 8000 🕐 Nightly

Walt Disney World and Lake Buena Vista

Copa Banana

Premiere Disney nightspot with a Caribbean flavour offering dancing, karaoke, and satellite TV for sports events.

✉ Disney's Dolphin Resort, 1500 Epcot Boulevard ☎ (407) 934 4000 🕐 Nightly

Copperfield Magic Underground

New for 1998, flamboyant magician David Copperfield opens a 30,000-square-foot theatrical restaurant at Disney-MGM Studios.

✉ Disney-MGM Studios, W Buena Vista Drive ☎ (407) 939 3463 🕐 Nightly

Nightclubs &
Discotheques

Orlando

Backstage at the Clarion
Live bands and DJs playing hits from the '70s through to the '90s at International Drive's only hotel nightclub.
✉ **Clarion Plaza Hotel, 9700 International Drive** ☎ **(407) 352 9700** 🕐 **Nightly until 2AM**
🚌 **I-Ride, Lynx #42**

Embassy Nightclub & Entertainment Complex
Multi-level dance floors, bar, plus games rooms, quiet areas and concert facilities.
✉ **5100 Adanson Street** ☎ **(407) 629 4779** 🕐 **Call for schedules**

Illusions Lounge
A late night bar with dancing. Latin nights on Thursdays and Saturdays from 9PM.
✉ **Orlando Marriott, 8001 International Drive** ☎ **(407) 351 2420** 🕐 **Nightly until 2AM**
🚌 **I-Ride, Lynx #42**

Phineas Phogg's
Lively discotheque in the Church Street Station complex (► 30–1) . Glitter ball, state-of-the-art lighting, live bands and DJ sessions. Minimum age 21.
✉ **Church Street Station (Exchange Building), 129 W Church Street** ☎ **(407) 422 2434** 🕐 **Sun–Thu until 1AM, Fri–Sat until 2AM**

Renaissance
Three-storey high-energy alternative dance club with live music and roof-top reggae; '80s Night on Tuesdays; Ladies' Night (free entry and drinks for women) on Wednesdays; Friday and Saturday are House Nights.
✉ **22 S Magnolia Avenue** ☎ **(407) 422 3595** 🕐 **Tue–Thu**
until 3AM, Fri–Sat until 4AM. Closed Sun–Mon

Walt Disney World and Lake Buena Vista

Baja Beach Club
Beach club-style party zone. Dancing, theme nights, limbo competitions, volleyball games and cocktails on the outdoor deck.
✉ **8510 Palm Parkway** ☎ **(407) 238 0088** 🕐 **Nightly until 2AM**

House of Blues
Nightclub-cum-live music venue featuring straight blues, R&B, jazz and country, plus a restaurant serving Delta-inspired cuisine. The LA original has been a huge success.
✉ **Downtown Disney** ☎ **(407) 934 2583** 🕐 **8AM–2AM (dining 11AM–2AM)**

Laughing Kookaburra Good Time Bar
Popular and often packed hotel nightclub with a small dance floor. Live music, Top 40 hits, speciality cocktails and a good atmosphere.
✉ **Buena Vista Palace Resort & Spa, 1900 Buena Vista Drive** ☎ **(407) 827 3722** 🕐 **Nightly until 2AM**

Pleasure Island
Three discotheques (STRAX, Mannequins and the Rock-n-Roll Beach Club) and four clubs, including comedy and country and western venues, crammed into Disney's top night-time entertainment complex (► 89).
✉ **Downtown Disney, E Buena Vista Drive** ☎ **(407) 934 7781** 🕐 **Nightly until 2AM**

It's The Law
Most discotheques and clubs admit under 18s as long as they are accompanied by an adult, though some insist on a minimum age of 21. Florida law prohibits the purchase or consumption of alcohol by anyone under 21. IDs are checked frequently, so any youthful-looking adults would be well advised to carry a passport or similar form of ID showing proof of their age. Everybody (regardless of seniority) must provide proof of age for admission to Pleasure Island.

What's on When

January
CompUSA Florida Citrus Bowl: nationally televised college football game on New Year's Day

February
International Carillon Festival: carillon concerts at Bok Tower Gardens
Silver Spurs Rodeo: major event on the Professional Rodeo Cowboys Association circuit held in Kissimmee
Daytona Speed Weeks: the Daytona 500 and more

March
Cypress Gardens Spring Flower Festival: award-winning floral displays (until May)
Kissimmee Blue Grass Festival: week-long toe-tapping music event
Winter Park Sidewalk Arts Festival: long weekend of art, food, music and activities

April
Pro Water Ski Tour and Wakeboard Series: waterbatics at Crane Roost Park, Altamonte Springs
Epcot International Flower & Garden Festival: garden and greenhouse tours, demonstrations and displays

May
Zellwood Sweet Corn Festival: 200,000 corn on the cobs get consumed over the weekend at this family event

June
Florida Film Festival: full-length movies, documentaries and shorts from around the world
A World of Orchids International Orchid Fair: thousands of orchids from growers worldwide

Silver Spurs Rodeo: the cowboys are back in Kissimmee

July
Lake Eola Picnic in the Park: Orlando celebrates the Fourth of July with games, activities and fireworks in Lake Eola Park

October
Walt Disney World/ Oldsmobile Golf Classic: top golfers gather for this annual PGA Tour event
Halloween: spooktacular special events at Church Street Station, Sea World, Silver Springs and Universal Studios

November
Orlando Magic Season Opener: the Magic open the basketball season
Cypress Gardens Mum (Chrysanthemum) Festival: 2.5 million blooms in spectacular horticultural displays
Annual Festival of the Masters: art show at Disney Village Marketplace

December
Cypress Gardens Poinsettia Festival & Garden of Lights: 400,000 lights and 40,000 poinsettias for Christmas
Mickey's Very Merry Christmas Party: yule celebrations at Magic Kingdom
Christmas in the Park: exhibition of Tiffany glass with seasonal music in downtown Winter Park
Church Street Station New Year's Eve Street Party
Night Before Citrus: music and laser shows at Sea World for the official Citrus Bowl New Year's Eve Party

Practical Matters

TIME DIFFERENCES

GMT	Orlando	Germany	USA (NY)	Netherlands	Spain
12 noon	← 7AM	→ 1PM	← 7AM	→ 1PM	→ 1PM

BEFORE YOU GO

WHAT YOU NEED

- ● Required
- ○ Suggested
- ▲ Not required

	UK	Germany	USA	Netherlands	Spain
Passport (valid for six months from date of entry)/National Identity Card	●	●	▲	●	●
Visa (waiver form to be completed)	▲	▲	▲	▲	▲
Onward or Return Ticket	●	●	▲	●	●
Health Inoculations (tetanus)	○	○	○	○	○
Health Documentation (reciprocal agreement) (► 123, Health)	▲	▲	▲	▲	▲
Travel Insurance	●	●	▲	●	●
Driving Licence (national or International Driving Permit)	●	●	●	●	●
Car Insurance Certificate	○	○	●	○	○
Car Registration Document	●	●	●	●	●

WHEN TO GO

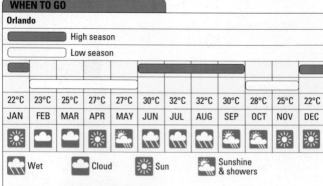

Orlando

High season

Low season

22°C	23°C	25°C	27°C	27°C	30°C	32°C	32°C	30°C	28°C	25°C	22°C
JAN	FEB	MAR	APR	MAY	JUN	JUL	AUG	SEP	OCT	NOV	DEC

Wet   Cloud   Sun   Sunshine & showers

TOURIST OFFICES

In the UK

Orlando Tourism Bureau
18–24 Westbourne Grove
London W2 5RH
☎ 0171 243 8072

The Kissimmee–St Cloud
Convention and Visitors
Bureau, Roebuck House
Palace Street
London SW1E 5BA
☎ 0171 630 1105

In the USA

The Orlando/Orange
County Visitors' Bureau
International Drive (at
corner of Austrian Court)
Orlando
☎ 407/363 5871

POLICE 911

FIRE 911

AMBULANCE 911

POLICE (NON EMERGENCY) 407/246 2414

WHEN YOU ARE THERE

ARRIVING

Orlando's international airport is one of the fastest growing in the US, with around 950 flights a day. Several international carriers fly direct into Orlando and many flights involve transfers to and from other US cities. The nearest alternative international gateway is Tampa, about an hour and a half from Orlando.

Orlando International Airport

Kilometres to city centre	Journey times	
	🚆	N/A
15 kilometres	🚌	45 minutes
	🚗	30 minutes

Tampa International Airport

Kilometres to city centre	Journey times	
	🚆	2 hours
137 kilometres	🚌	2 hours
	🚗	90 minutes

MONEY

An unlimited amount of American dollars can be imported or exported, but amounts of over £10,000 must be reported to US Customs, as should similar amounts of gold. US dollars traveller's cheques ('checks' in America) are accepted as cash in most places (not taxis) as are credit cards, (Amex, Visa, Mastercard, Diners Card). Dollar bills come in 1, 2, 5, 10, 20, 50 and 100 denominations. Note that all dollar bills are the same size and colour – all greenbacks. One dollar is made up of 100 cents. Coins are of 1 cent (pennies), 5 cents (nickel), 10 cents (dime) and 25 cents (quarter).

TIME

Orlando local time is Eastern Standard Time (the same as New York) which is five hours behind Greenwich Mean Time (GMT–5). Daylight saving applies, with clocks one hour ahead between April and October.

CUSTOMS

 YES

There are duty-free allowances for non-US residents over 21 years of age:

Alcohol: spirits (over 22% volume):	1L
Wine:	1L
Cigarettes:	200 *or*
Cigars:	50 *or*
Tobacco:	2kg
Duty-free gifts:	$100

provided the stay in US is at least 72 hours and that gift exemption has not been claimed in the previous six months. There are no currency limits.

 NO

Meat or meat products, dairy products, fruits, seeds, drugs, lottery tickets or obscene publications.
Never carry a bag through Customs for anyone else.

CONSULATES

UK
☎ 407/426 7855

Germany
☎ 305/358 0290
(Miami)

Netherlands
☎ 407/425 8000

Spain
☎ 305/358 1992
(Spanish Tourist Office, Miami)

WHEN YOU ARE THERE

TOURIST OFFICES

Orlando/Orange County Convention and Visitors Bureau Inc
● 6700 Forum Drive
Suite 100
Orlando,
Florida 32821-8087
☎ 407/363 5822
Fax: 407/370 5002

Official Visitor Centre
● 8723 International Drive
Suite 101
Orlando, Florida 32819
☎ 407/363 5872
Open all year 8AM–8PM.

Tourist Information 'Know Before You Go'
● ☎ Toll free from USA
(800) 749 1993
☎ (outside US) 407/396 5400

There are Central Florida Full Service Tourist Information Centres at:
Orlando
● 8000 International Drive
(Suite 9)
Highway 1–4 Exit 29

● Shell Oil Service Centre Highway 1–4 to Exit 29 – Sea World, Universal & Wet and Wild (corner of 1–4 and Sand Lake Road, next to Checkers)

Kissimmee
● Tourist Information 'Know Before You Go'
4720 W Highway 192
(next to Citrus House, just east of Special Tee Golf)

Most hotels have service desks or brochure racks.

NATIONAL HOLIDAYS

J	F	M	A	M	J	J	A	S	O	N	D
2	1	(1)	(1)	1		1		1	1	2	1

1 Jan	New Year's Day
Jan (third Mon)	Martin Luther King Day
Feb (third Mon)	Washington's Birthday
Mar/Apr	Good Friday
May (last Mon)	Memorial Day
4 Jul	Independence Day
Sep (first Mon)	Labor Day
Oct (second Mon)	Columbus Day
11 Nov	Veterans' Day
Nov (fourth Thu)	Thanksgiving
25 Dec	Christmas Day

Boxing Day is not a public holiday in the US. Some shops open on National Holidays.

OPENING HOURS

○ Shops	● Post Offices
● Offices	● Museums
● Banks	● Pharmacies

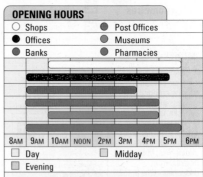

| 8AM | 9AM | 10AM | NOON | 2PM | 3PM | 4PM | 5PM | 6PM |

☐ Day   ☐ Midday   ▨ Evening

There are two all-night pharmacies: Ekered Drugs, 908 Lee Road, and Walgreen Drug Store, International Drive (opposite Wet and Wild). Some shops in malls and on International Drive open until 9PM. Post offices are few and far between; hotels are usually helpful with postal matters. Banks, offices and post offices close on Saturday. Opening times of theme parks vary with seasonal demand. Opening times of museums vary; check with individual museum. Many museums are closed on Monday.

DRIVE ON THE
RIGHT

TOILETS
FREE

PUBLIC TRANSPORT

 Air Orlando is a major domestic and an international airport. There are non-stop flights from about 70 different US destinations, in addition to more than 100 cities worldwide. It is easily accessible and within 24km of major attractions, such as Walt Disney World, and downtown Orlando. Airport ☎ 407/825 2001.

 Trains Amtrak trains serve Orlando with four daily trains originating in New York, Tampa and Miami, also stopping at Winter Park and Sanford, north of the city, and Kissimmee near Walt Disney World. Amtrak offers an Auto Train overnight service with sleepers, which conveys passengers with their cars and vans, and runs daily between Lorton Va, and Sanford, Fa. For general information ☎ 1 800 872 7245 (toll-free).

 Buses Greyhound lines serve Orlando from many centres in the US: within the metropolitan area local buses provide a good service, notably Gray Line, which serves the airport and most of Orlando's main attractions and hotels. Greyhound bus ☎ 407/292 3422. For excursions around the area and to the major attractions, tour companies offer diverse itineraries or can customise trips for groups.

 Urban Transport Besides taxi and limousine service to anywhere in the Greater Orlando area, the city's Lynx bus system provides economical public transportation around Orlando. Bus stops are marked with a 'paw' print of a Lynx cat. The I-ride buses serve International Drive, with stops every 5–10 minutes. The stops are marked 'I-RIDE' at each Lynx bus stop.

CAR RENTAL

 Rates are very competitive. Take an unlimited mileage deal, collision damage waiver and adequate (more than minimal) insurance. There is a surcharge on drivers under 25 and the minimum age is often 21 (sometimes 25). Expect to pay by credit card.

TAXIS

 Rates are expensive (around $2.50 for the first mile and around $1.50 for each additional mile). If money is no object, limousine transport can be easily arranged through your hotel's guest services desk.

DRIVING

 Speed limit on interstate highways **88–104kph**

 Speed limits on main roads: **88–104kph**

 Speed limits on urban roads: **32–88kph**. All speed limits are strictly enforced.

 Must be worn by drivers and front-seat passengers. Children under three must use child safety seats; older children must use a safety seat or seat belt.

 There are tough drinking and driving laws. Limit: 0.08 per cent of alcohol in blood.

 Fuel (*gasoline*), is cheaper in America than in Europe. It is sold in American gallons (five American gallons equal 18 litres), and comes in three grades, all unleaded. Many gas stations have automatic vending machines that accept notes and major credit cards.

 If you break down pull over, raise the bonnet (hood), switch on the hazard lights, and call the rental company or the breakdown number, which should be displayed on or near the dashboard. The American Automobile Association (AAA) provides certain reciprocal facilities to affiliated motoring organisations in other countries. For AAA breakdown assistance ☎ 1 800 222 4357 (toll free).

PERSONAL SAFETY

Orlando is not generally a dangerous place but to help prevent crime and accidents:

- Never open your hotel room door unless you know who is there. If in doubt call hotel security.
- Place valuables in a safety deposit box.
- Always lock your front and/or patio doors when in the room and when leaving. Use the safety chain/lock for security.
- When driving, keep all car doors locked.
- Never approach alligators, they can outrun a man.

Police assistance:
☎ **091**
from any call box

TELEPHONES

There are telephones in hotel lobbies, drug stores, restaurants, garages and at the roadside. A local call costs 25 cents. Buy cards for long distance calls from the Official Visitors Centre, some pharmacies and grocery stores. Dial '0' for the operator. 'Collect' means reverse the charges.

International Dialling Codes	
From Orlando (US) to:	
UK:	011 44
Ireland:	011 353
Australia:	011 61
Germany:	011 49
Netherlands:	011 31
Spain:	011 34

POST

Post offices in Orlando are few and far between. Stamps from vending machines are sold at a 25 per cent premium; it is best to buy them at your hotel. Letters to UK are $1, postcards 46 cents. Post offices are usually open Mon–Fri 9AM–5PM, but many hotels and major attractions provide a post office service out of hours.

ELECTRICITY

The power supply is: 110/120 volts AC (60 cycles)

Type of socket: sockets take two-prong, flat-pin plugs.

Visitors should bring adaptors for their 3-pin and 2-round-pin plugs.

TIPS/GRATUITIES

Yes ✓ No ✗		
It is useful to have plenty of small notes		
Hotels (chambermaid, doorman etc)	✓	$1
Restaurants (waiter, waitresses	✓	15/20%
Bar Service	✓	15%
Taxis	✓	15%
Tour guides (discretionary)	✓	
Porters	✓	$1 per bag
Hairdressers	✓	15%
Toilets (rest rooms)	✗	

PHOTOGRAPHY

What to photograph: Orlando and its nearby theme parks are great places to take photographs. There are plenty of opportunities for classic Disney shots, as well as those of natural flora and fauna.

When to photograph: The hot summer months can be very humid and may affect photography. The best time of day to photograph is between 1 and 6pm.

Where to buy film: All types of film and photo processing are freely available in drugstores, theme parks etc but it is cheaper to take your own film.

HEALTH

Insurance

Medical insurance cover of at least $1,000,000 unlimited cover is strongly recommended, as medical bills can be astronomical and treatment may be withheld if you have no evidence of means to pay.

Dental Services

Your medical insurance cover should include dental treatment, which is readily available, but expensive. Have a check up before you go. Dental referral telephone numbers are in the Yellow Pages telephone directory or ask at the desk of your hotel.

Sun Advice

By far the most common source of ill health in Florida is too much sun. Orlando in summer is very hot and humid and the sun is strong all year round. Use a sunscreen, wear a hat outdoors and ensure that everyone drinks plenty of fluids.

Drugs

Medicines can be bought at drug stores, certain drugs generally available elsewhere require a prescription in the US. Acetaminophen is the US equivalent of paracetamol. Take an insect repellent including Deet and cover up after dark, to avoid being bitten by mosquitoes.

Safe Water

Restaurants usually provide a jug of iced water. Drinking unboiled water from taps is safe but not advisable. Mineral water is cheap and readily available.

CONCESSIONS

Students/Youths Most concessions at major theme parks apply to children under 17, but some sights and attractions offer special admission prices to bona fide students. There are also concessionary rail fares (International Student Identity Card required as proof).

Senior Citizens (Seniors) Over three million mature travellers visit Orlando each year, in addition to the 'Senior' permanent residents, and many special discounts are available to those over 55. Members of the American Association of Retired Persons, over 50 (AARPs) are eligible (with ID) for discounts on accommodation, meals, car rental, transport and many attractions in the Orlando area.

CLOTHING SIZES

Orlando (USA)	UK	Rest of Europe
Suits		
36	36	46
38	38	48
40	40	50
42	42	52
44	44	54
46	46	56
Shoes		
8	7	41
8.5	7.5	42
9.5	8.5	43
10.5	9.5	44
11.5	10.5	45
12	11	46
Shirts		
15	15	38
15.5	15.5	39/40
16	16	41
16.5	16.5	42
17	17	43
Dresses		
8	6	34
10	8	36
12	10	38
14	12	40
16	14	42
18	16	44
Shoes		
6	4.5	38
6.5	5	38
7	5.5	39
7.5	6	39
8	6.5	40
8.5	7	41

WHEN DEPARTING

- Check airport terminal number (there are three terminals) and allow plenty of time to get there and hand in any rental car.
- Arrive at check-in at least two hours before departure time.
- US Customs are strict. There are no departure taxes but ensure that you have all necessary documentation and that you are not contravening US Customs regulations.

LANGUAGE

The official language of the USA is English, and, given that one third of all overseas visitors come from the UK, Orlando natives have few problems coping with British accents and dialects. Spanish is also widely spoken, as large numbers of Latin American immigrants work in the hotel and catering industries. However, many English words have different meanings and below are some words in common usage where they differ from the English spoken in the UK:

holiday	*vacation*	tap	*faucet*
fortnight	*two weeks*	refrigerator	*icebox*
ground floor	*first floor*	luggage	*baggage*
first floor	*second floor*	suitcase	*valise*
second floor	*third floor*	hotel porter	*bellhop*
flat	*apartment*	chambermaid	*room maid*
lift	*elevator*	surname	*last name*
eiderdown	*comforter*	cupboard	*closet*

cheque	*check*	25 cent coin	*quarter*
traveller's	*traveler's*	banknote	*bill*
cheque	*check*	banknote (collo-	*greenback*
I cent coin	*penny*	quial)	
5 cent coin	*nickel*	dollar (colloquial)	*buck*
10 cent coin	*dime*	cashpoint	*automatic teller*

grilled	*broiled*	biscuit	*cookie*
frankfurter	*frank*	scone	*biscuit*
prawns	*shrip*	sorbet	*sherbet*
aubergine	*eggplant*	jelly	*jello*
courgette	*zucchini*	jam	*jelly*
maize	*corn*	confectionery	*candy*
chips (potato)	*fries*	spirit	*liquor*
crisps (potato)	*chips*	soft drink	*soda*

car	*automobile*	petrol	*gas, gasoline*
bonnet (of car)	*hood*	railway	*railroad, railway*
boot (of car)	*trunk*	tram	*streetcar*
repair	*fix*	underground	*subway*
caravan	*trailer*	platform	*track*
lorry	*truck*	buffer	*bumper*
motorway	*freeway*	single ticket	*one-way ticket*
main road	*highway*	return ticket	*round-trip ticket*

shop	*store*	policeman	*cop*
chemist (shop)	*drugstore*	post	*mail*
cinema	*movies*	post code	*zip code*
pavement	*sidewalk*	ring up,	*call*
subway	*underpass*	telephone	
gangway	*aisle*	long-distance	*trunk call*
toilet	*rest room*	call	
trousers	*pants*	autumn	*fall*
nappy	*diaper*	gangway	*aisle*
glasses	*eyeglasses*	pavement	*sidewalk*

Acknowledgements

The Automobile Association wishes to thank the following libraries and organisations for their assistance in the preparation of this book:

BUSCH ENTERTAINMENT GROUP 27a, 48a; BRUCE COLEMAN COLLECTION 12a; KENNEDY SPACE CENTER 11; KISSIMMEE & ST CLOUD C & VB 9b, 55; LEU GARDENS 13; MARY EVANS PICTURE LIBRARY 10, 14; MRI BANKER'S GUIDE TO FOREIGN CURRENCY 119; P MURPHY 12b, 50, 63; NATURE PHOTOGRAPHERS 61 (P R Sterry); ORLANDO & ORANGE COUNTY C & VB B/cover: oranges, 7a, 17, 19, 30/1, 34, 91b; PICTURES COLOUR LIBRARY 8b, 22; RIPLEY'S BELIEVE IT OR NOT! 35; SPECTRUM COLOUR LIBRARY 16, 27b, 48b, 49; SEA WORLD 15a, 38/9a, 38/9b; UNIVERSAL STUDIOS 26, 41a; THE WALT DISNEY CO. 25, 68, 71, 74/5, 76/7, 80/1, 82/3, 87, 89, 90; WET N' WILD 1; WORLD PICTURES F/cover (a): downtown Orlando.

The remaining photographs are held in the Association's own library (AA PHOTO LIBRARY) and were taken by Tony Souter, with the exception of the following:
P Bennett F/cover (b) spaceman, 7b, 15b, 20, 21, 47, 60, 62, 66, 117b.

The author would like to thank Jayne Teleska Behrle, Orlando-Orange County Convention and Visitors Bureau, Inc; Hayley Busse, Orlando-Orange County Convention and Visitors Bureau, UK; Larry White, Kissimmee-St Cloud Convention and Visitors Bureau, USA; Sarah Handy, Kissimmee-St Cloud Convention and Visitors Bureau, UK; and Joyce Taylor, Walt Disney Attractions, UK.

Contributors

Copy editor: Nia Williams   Page Layout: Barfoot Design   Verifier: Paul Murphy
Researcher (Practical Matters): Lesley Allard   Indexer: Marie Lorimer

Dear Essential Traveller

Your comments, opinions and recommendations are very important to us. So please help us to improve our travel guides by taking a few minutes to complete this simple questionnaire.

You do not need a stamp (unless posted outside the UK). If you do not want to cut this page from your guide, then photocopy it or write your answers on a plain sheet of paper.

Send to: **The Editor, AA World Travel Guides, FREEPOST SCE 4598, Basingstoke RG21 4GY.**

Your recommendations...

We always encourage readers' recommendations for restaurants, nightlife or shopping – if your recommendation is used in the next edition of the guide, we will send you a **FREE AA Essential Guide** of your choice. Please state below the establishment name, location and your reasons for recommending it.

_____

_____

_____

_____

Please send me **AA Essential**
(see list of titles inside the front cover)

_____

About this guide...

Which title did you buy?

AA Essential _____

Where did you buy it?

_____

When? $\underline{m\,m}$ / $\underline{y\,y}$

Why did you choose an AA *Essential* Guide?

_____

_____

_____

_____

Did this guide meet your expectations?

Exceeded ☐ Met all ☐ Met most ☐ Fell below ☐

Please give your reasons

_____

_____

_____

_____

continued on next page...

Were there any aspects of this guide that you particularly liked?

_____

_____

_____

Is there anything we could have done better?

_____

_____

_____

_____

_____

About you...

Name (Mr/Mrs/Ms) _____

Address _____

_____

Postcode _____

Daytime tel nos _____

Which age group are you in?
Under 25 ☐ 25-34 ☐ 35-44 ☐ 45-54 ☐ 55-64 ☐ 65+ ☐

How many trips do you make a year?
Less than one ☐ One ☐ Two ☐ Three or more ☐

Are you an AA member? Yes ☐ No ☐

About your trip...

When did you book? mm / yy When did you travel? mm / yy

How long did you stay? _____

Was it for business or leisure? _____

Did you buy any other travel guides for your trip?

If yes, which ones? _____

_____

Thank you for taking the time to complete this questionnaire. Please send it to us as soon as possible, and remember, you do not need a stamp (unless posted outside the UK).

Happy Holidays!